# SHOPPING MATTERS 1

## Englisch für Einzelhandelskaufleute



von
**Maria Elisabeth Köstler**

Cornelsen

*Shopping Matters* wurde geplant und entwickelt von der Verlagsredaktion
der Cornelsen und Oxford University Press GmbH & Co., Berlin.

| | |
|---|---|
| *Verfasserin:* | Maria Elisabeth Köstler, Wien |
| *Verlagsredaktion:* | Janan Barksdale |
| *Redaktionelle Mitarbeit:* | Sigrid Janssen, Fritz Preuss, Catherine Richmond, Leah Williams |
| *Bildredaktion:* | Uta Hübner |
| *Umschlagfoto:* | Comstock Fotoagentur |
| *Gesamtgestaltung und technische Umsetzung:* | Oxford Designers & Illustrators |

**Quellenverzeichnis**

**Grafiken:** Oxford Designers & Illustrators

**Fotos: J. Austin**: S. 15 (2), 22 (2), 38 (3); **J. Barksdale**: S. 15 (2), 22 (4), 38 (13), 80; **BAVARIA Bildagentur**: S. 11/Kappelmeyer, PP; 21/Hasselmeier; 33/VCL; 63/S. Corro; 88/VCL; **Christoph Buckstegen**: S. 8, 12, 15, 22, 40, 42, 57, 62, 80, 81, 87; **Jan Chipps Photography**: S. 6, 8 (2), 24, 26 (8), 34 (7), 44, 66, 67; **COMSTOCK**: S. 8 (3), 15 (8), 22 (9), 32, 38 (3), 52, 77 (8), 78 (4), 83; **Das Fotoarchiv**: S. 72/T. Mayer; **Hubert Herr GmbH**: S. 58; **U. Hübner**: S. 54 (2), 68 (3); **The Image Bank**: S. 51/DeLossy; **IFA-Bilderteam**: S. 16/Erniecomp; 51/B. Welsh; **Swarovski (Deutschland) GmbH**, Kaufbeuren: S. 57 (2)

Erhältlich sind auch:
Audio-CD (Best.-Nr. 23591)
Lehrerhandreichung (Best.–Nr. 23583)

**www.cornelsen.de**

1. Auflage, 7. Druck 2007/06

Alle Drucke dieser Auflage sind inhaltlich unverändert und
können im Unterricht nebeneinander verwendet werden.



Druck: CS-Druck CornelsenStürtz, Berlin

ISBN 978-3-8109-2357-8

Inhalt gedruckt auf säurefreiem Papier aus nachhaltiger Forstwirtschaft.

# Vorwort

*Shopping Matters* ist ein neues, zweibändiges Lehrwerk für Einzelhandelskaufleute, die am Berufsschulunterricht oder an betrieblichen Fortbildungsmaßnahmen teilnehmen. Das Werk basiert auf den Lehrplänen der Berufsschulen. Der erste Band des Lehrwerks setzt nur geringfügige Englischkenntnisse voraus.

*Shopping Matters Band 1* besteht aus 12 Units sowie einer kurzen Übungseinheit zur englischen Geschäftskorrespondenz. In jeder Unit werden die Lernenden in berufsbezogenen Situationen mit allen wesentlichen Aspekten des Englischen vertraut gemacht. Es ist möglich, einzelne Units auszulassen, jedoch wird empfohlen, wann immer Zeit und Lehrpläne es erlauben, die gegebene Reihenfolge einzuhalten, um einen kontinuierlichen Aufbau des Fachvokabulars und der grammatikalischen Strukturen zu gewährleisten.

*Shopping Matters* bietet die Möglichkeit eines handlungsorientierten wie auch eines praxisbezogenen Unterrichts. Die Lernenden schulen aktiv ihre Sprechfertigkeit in Rollenspielen und in Partnerarbeit, wobei neben der beruflichen auch die soziale Komponente des Arbeitsalltags einbezogen wird. Grammatik spielt eine untergeordnete Rolle. Erklärungen von Regeln und Übungen sind zwar vorhanden, jedoch auf das Wesentliche begrenzt.

*Shopping Matters Band 1* enthält drei Wortlisten: eine chronologische Liste, eine alphabetische Liste, eine Grundwortschatzliste von ca. 400 Wörtern, die als bekannt vorausgesetzt werden. Der Anhang enthält darüber hinaus sowohl die *Transcripts* für die Hörverstehensübungen als auch die *Pairwork files* mit den Angaben für die *Information-gap*-Übungen bzw. Rollenspiele.

Der Verlag und die Autorin wünschen Ihnen viel Erfolg und Freude bei der Arbeit mit *Shopping Matters*.

Maria Elisabeth Köstler

🎧 Dieses Symbol weist darauf hin, dass sich der Text bzw. Dialog auf der Audio-CD befindet.

# Contents

UNIT

# 1 A new job

## 1 Who's who?

Hello, my name is Emily Jones. I'm 17 years old and I live in England. I'm a trainee at SNIPS supermarket in London. The manager is Mrs Deborah Wood.

MRS WOOD Harry, could you show Emily round the shop and introduce her to the others, please? I'm a bit busy at the moment.

HARRY Hello, you're the new trainee, aren't you? My name is Harry Osborne. I'm one of the shop assistants.

EMILY Hi, Harry. I'm Emily Jones.

HARRY Let me introduce you to some of the other people here.

EMILY Okay. Who's that woman over there?

HARRY That's Rhaina Panjabi. She's our window dresser. She comes once a week to dress our shop windows. Come on, I'll introduce you to her. Emily, this is Rhaina Panjabi. Rhaina, this is Emily Jones.

EMILY Hello, Rhaina.

RHAINA Hello. Welcome to your new place of work.

EMILY Who's the woman on the checkout?

HARRY That's Fiona Williams, a cashier.

EMILY And the guy over there?

HARRY That's another trainee, Jason North. He finishes his training next year. Come on, let's go and meet him. Emily, this is Jason North. Jason, this is Emily Jones, our new colleague.

JASON Hi, Emily. Welcome to SNIPS.

EMILY Hi, Jason.

HARRY So, I think you know most of the people now.

EMILY Right, thank you.

JASON Um, could you help me with these boxes, Emily?

EMILY Of course. See you later, Harry.

Now say who works at SNIPS supermarket. What are their jobs?

GRAMMAR CHECK

## SIMPLE PRESENT: statements and the verb 'to be'

*1* I'**m** (= I **am**) Emily Jones.
*2* She'**s** (= She **is**) our window dresser.
*3* She **comes** once a week to dress our shop windows.

- *Die einfache Gegenwart* (simple present) *wird verwendet für gleich bleibende Zustände (1, 2) und regelmäßige, wiederholte Handlungen (3). Bei* he/she/it *wird in der Regel (wie z. B. bei* come *oder* work*) -s an die Grundform angehängt (3). Vorsicht aber bei dem Verb* to be *(1, 2).*

**Statements** – *Aussagen*

| **work** | **be** | |
|---|---|---|
| I work | I am | (I'm) |
| you work | you are | (you're) |
| he/she/it works | he/she/it is | (he's/she's/it's) |
| we work | we are | (we're) |
| you work | you are | (you're) |
| they work | they are | (they're) |

**Questions** – *Fragen* / **Negatives** – *Verneinungen*

| **be** | **be** | |
|---|---|---|
| am I? | I am not | (I'm not) |
| are you? | you are not | (you're not) |
| is he/she/it? | he/she/it is not | (he/she/it isn't) |
| are we? | we are not | (we're not) |
| are you? | you are not | (you're not) |
| are they? | they are not | (they're not) |

⚠ May *(dürfen),* can *(können) und* could *(könnte[n]) sind für alle Personen gleich.*

**May** I help you?
He **can** speak English but he **can't** (= cannot) speak French.
**Could** you show Emily round the shop?

## 2 Introductions

Work with a partner to introduce yourself. The following words may help you:

| | |
|---|---|
| Hi, my name is ... | Hello, I'm ... |
| I'm ... . Pleased to meet you. | My name is ... . Pleased to meet you. |
| How do you do? | How do you do? |

## 3 People at SNIPS

Copy the table below in your exercise book. Listen to the CD and fill it in.

Deborah Wood

Harry Osborne

Beatrice Anderson

Jason North

Rhaina Panjabi

Fiona Williams

| name | job (or who they are) | what they do |
|---|---|---|
| *Deborah Wood* | *manager* | *runs the shop* |

## 4 Practice

Write full sentences about the people at SNIPS.

EXAMPLE *Mrs Wood is the manager. She runs the shop. She is very busy.*

## 5 What about you?

Describe your job and the people at your place of work.

## 6 Practice

Rewrite the sentences with the correct verb form.

*1* Emily ... (be) a trainee.
*2* I ... (be) also a trainee.
*3* She ... (live) in London.
*4* Harry ... (be) a shop assistant.
*5* Rhaina ... (not be) a shop assistant.
*6* She ... (be) a window dresser.
*7* She ... (like) her job.
*8* You ... (not be) a window dresser.
*9* Fiona ... (work) on the checkout.
*10* Jason and Emily ... (be) trainees.
*11* They ... (work) at SNIPS.
*12* Emily ... (know) most of the people now.
*13* We also ... (know) most of the people now.
*14* Emily ... (help) Jason with the boxes.

GRAMMAR CHECK

### THE VERB 'TO BE': negative questions and short answers

**Negative questions** – *verneinte Fragen*

| | |
|---|---|
| Aren't you the new trainee? | – Yes, I am. |
| Isn't he the manager? | – No, he isn't. Mrs Wood is. |

**Short answers** – *Kurzantworten*

| | |
|---|---|
| Yes, I am. | No, I am not. |
| Yes, you are. | No, you aren't. |
| Yes, he/she/it is. | No, he/she/it isn't. |
| Yes, we are. | No, we aren't. |
| Yes, you are. | No, you aren't. |
| Yes, they are. | No, they aren't. |

## 7 Practice

Give short answers.

EXAMPLE Is Emily a trainee? *Yes, she is.*

1. Is Mrs Wood the manager?
2. Isn't Emily a manager?
3. Are Emily and Fiona women?
4. Are you a manager?
5. Are you all trainees?
6. Are you all window dressers?
7. Isn't Jason a trainee?
8. Is Harry a cashier?
9. Is Emily good-looking?
10. Aren't Harry and Jason good-looking?

## 8 A or an?

Put in *a* or *an*.

1. ... shop
2. ... English shop
3. ... cashier
4. ... young man
5. ... old man
6. ... apple
7. ... green apple
8. ... assistant
9. ... shop assistant
10. ... European country
11. ... supermarket
12. ... Austrian supermarket

### A OR AN?

| | |
|---|---|
| a + *Konsonant* | a colleague, a trainee |
| an + *Vokal* | an orange, an apple |

*Aber:* an hour, a university *(Aussprache!)*

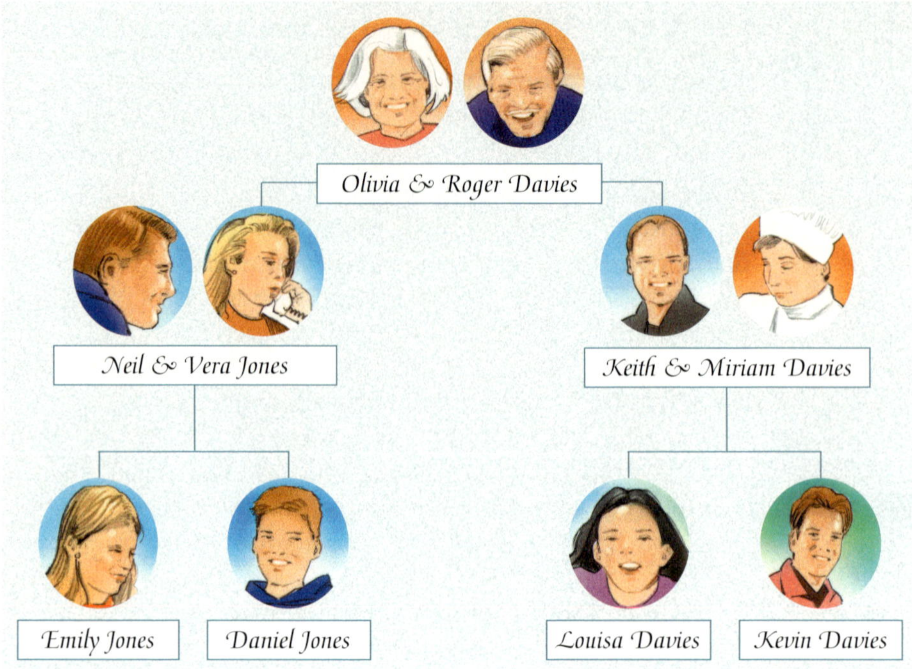


## 9 Who's who?

Look at Emily's family tree and complete the text.

aunt ◆ brother ◆ cousins ◆ daughter-in-law ◆ granddaughter ◆ grandfather ◆ parents ◆ sister ◆ uncle

Neil and Vera are my ...1, Daniel is my ...2 and I am his ...3. Olivia is my grandmother and Roger is my ...4 . Keith is my mother's brother so he is my ...5. Miriam is his wife so she is my ...6. Louisa and Kevin are my ...7. Miriam is Olivia and Roger's ...8 and I am their ...9.

## 10 Who am I?

Look at the sentences and find out who is talking.

1. I've got four grandchildren and I'm married to Roger.
2. I've got a sister and Keith is my father.
3. I've got two children, just like my sister Vera.
4. Daniel is my grandson and Olivia is my wife.
5. I'm Keith's nephew.
6. I am Daniel's sister.
7. I've got two cousins and I'm Vera's niece.
8. I've got a niece and a nephew and Keith is my husband.
9. I'm Miriam's mother-in-law.
10. I've got a son and a daughter and Keith is my brother.

## 11 What are their jobs?

Complete the text using the words below:

cook ◆ hairdresser ◆ housewife ◆ gardener ◆ carpenter ◆ nurse ◆ plumber ◆ office clerk ◆ mechanic

My father is an ...1 and works for an insurance company. My mother is a ...2 at St. Anne's hospital. My brother Daniel still goes to school. He is very interested in woodwork and wants to become a ...3. Uncle Keith is a ...4, he installs central heating systems. Aunt Miriam works as a ...5 in the canteen of a big company. My cousin Louisa goes to school. She says she wants to become a ...6 because she likes doing people's hair. But who knows, she is only 12. Her brother Kevin is a ...7, he repairs cars. My grandmother is a ...8 (she works at home) and my grandfather is a ...9. He is retired now but he still works in his own back garden and knows everything about flowers and plants.

## 12 My family

Draw your family tree and tell your partner about it.

## 13 Puzzle

Copy this table onto a separate piece of paper. Then fill it in with words from the puzzle.

| jobs | family members |
|---|---|
| | |
| | |

| | | | | | | | | | | | | | | | | | | | |
|---|---|---|---|---|---|---|---|---|---|---|---|---|---|---|---|---|---|---|---|
| B | O | F | F | I | C | E | C | L | E | R | K | R | I | S | B | O | L | E | D |
| C | A | C | W | I | N | D | O | W | D | R | E | S | S | E | R | F | S | M | A |
| H | N | U | R | S | E | B | U | N | R | O | E | Q | U | R | O | W | A | N | U |
| I | D | A | E | L | I | D | S | E | C | W | C | E | N | T | T | O | U | T | G |
| L | N | E | P | H | E | W | I | R | O | I | U | O | E | R | H | S | N | R | H |
| D | I | U | S | F | N | H | N | A | A | F | S | E | O | S | E | E | C | O | T |
| R | E | G | T | O | S | F | V | I | P | E | N | U | M | K | R | G | L | A | E |
| E | C | G | R | A | N | D | F | A | T | H | E | R | F | A | I | T | E | N | R |
| N | E | H | C | M | P | L | U | M | B | E | R | I | P | S | E | R | N | X | O |
| A | N | A | U | N | T | O | S | H | O | P | A | S | S | I | S | T | A | N | T |

UNIT

# 2 At a grocery shop

## 1 Excuse me, do you speak English?

Jason North is in Hamburg for the weekend. He is in a grocery shop and would like to buy some things but he doesn't speak German.

JASON Excuse me, do you speak English?
PETRA Yes, a little. What can I do for you?
JASON How much are these pretzels? There's no price on them.
PETRA They're 75 cents each. How many would you like?
JASON Two please.
PETRA Certainly sir. Anything else?
JASON Yes, some milk. How much is a bottle of milk?
PETRA A one litre bottle is 85 cents and a half litre bottle is 45 cents.
JASON I'll have a half litre bottle please. And have you got any oranges?
PETRA No, I'm sorry, we haven't. But we've got apples and bananas.
JASON How much are the bananas?
PETRA They are €1.20 a kilogram. Would you like some?
JASON Yes, three please.
PETRA Here you are, sir. That's 450 grams. Anything else?
JASON No, thank you, that's all. Where do I pay?
PETRA At the checkout, over there.

Answer the questions.

1 What does Jason ask for?
2 What does he buy?
3 How much are the bananas?
4 Where does he pay?

GRAMMAR CHECK

### SIMPLE PRESENT: questions, negatives and 'have got'

*1* **Do** you **speak** English?
*2* Jason **doesn't speak** German.
*3* We**'ve got** apples and bananas.
*4* **Have** you **got** any oranges? – No, I'm sorry, we **haven't.** / Yes, we **have**.

- *Fragen und Verneinungen werden meist (wie bei* speak *und* work*) mit dem Hilfsverb* do *bzw. in der 3. Person Singular mit der Form* does *gebildet (1, 2). Vorsicht aber bei den Verben* be *(siehe Seite 7) und* have got *(3, 4).*

**work**

| **Questions** – *Fragen* | **Negatives** – *Verneinungen* |
|---|---|
| do I work? | I do not (= don't) work |
| do you work? | you do not (= don't) work |
| does he/she/it work? | he/she/it does not (= doesn't) work |
| do we work? | we do not (= don't) work |
| do you work? | you do not (= don't) work |
| do they work? | they do not (= don't) work |

**have got**

| **Statements** | **Questions** | **Negatives** |
|---|---|---|
| I have got | have I got? | I haven't got |
| you have got | have you got? | you haven't got |
| he/she/it has got | has he/she/it got? | he/she/it hasn't got |
| we have got | have we got? | we haven't got |
| you have got | have you got? | you haven't got |
| they have got | have they got? | they haven't got |

⚠ Americans, and sometimes Britons, say:

**Do** you **have** ... ? – Yes, I **do**. / No, I **don't**.

## 2 Practice

Rewrite the sentences using the correct verb form.

*1* Emily and Jason ... (live) in London.
*2* We ... (not live) in London.
*3* ... (you want) to live in London?
*4* Harry and Rhaina ... (like) their jobs.
*5* ... (you like) your job?
*6* Harry ... (work) at the deli counter.
*7* ... (Mrs Anderson come) every day?
*8* Rhaina ... (come) once a week.
*9* Emily ... (not work) on the checkout.
*10* I ... (speak) English.
*11* I ... (not speak) Spanish.
*12* Jason ... (not speak) German.

## 3 Questions and answers

Find the matching questions and answers. Write them down on a separate piece of paper.

| | | |
|---|---|---|
| 1 What | do you get up in the morning? | Once a week. |
| 2 Which | can I do for you? | She is our new colleague. |
| 3 How much | is the girl over there? | Because it's a good supermarket. |
| 4 When | does she decorate the shop windows? | In London. |
| 5 Who | do you go shopping at SNIPS? | At 7. |
| 6 How often | does she live? | The one with chocolate, please. |
| 7 Where | one would you like? | I'd like a doughnut, please. |
| 8 Why | is it? | €1.20. |

### MUCH / MANY

| **much** *(viel)* | **many** *(viele)* |
|---|---|
| *(für unzählbare Begriffe)* | *(für zählbare Begriffe)* |
| milk | apples |
| coffee | bottles |

## 4 Much or many?

Put in *much* or *many*.

*1* … time
*2* … minutes
*3* … coins
*4* … money
*5* … supermarkets
*6* … work
*7* … trainees
*8* … checkouts
*9* … water
*10* … glasses of water
*11* … sunshine
*12* … rain
*13* … teacups
*14* … tea
*15* … orange juice
*16* … oranges

### TELLING A CUSTOMER THE PRICE

| | | | |
|---|---|---|---|
| How much | is | an apple? | |
| How much | does | an apple | cost? |
| It's (= it is) | 55 cents. | | |
| It costs | 55 cents. | | |
| How much | are | the oranges? | |
| How much | do | the carrots | cost? |
| They are | 1 euro 25 | a kilogram. | |
| They cost | 85 cents | each. | |

## CARDINAL NUMBERS

| | | | | | |
|---|---|---|---|---|---|
| **1** | one | **15** | fifteen | **29** | twenty-nine |
| **2** | two | **16** | sixteen | **30** | thirty |
| **3** | three | **17** | seventeen | **40** | forty |
| **4** | four | **18** | eighteen | **50** | fifty |
| **5** | five | **19** | nineteen | **60** | sixty |
| **6** | six | **20** | twenty | **70** | seventy |
| **7** | seven | **21** | twenty-one | **80** | eighty |
| **8** | eight | **22** | twenty-two | **90** | ninety |
| **9** | nine | **23** | twenty-three | **100** | one hundred |
| **10** | ten | **24** | twenty-four | **101** | one hundred and one |
| **11** | eleven | **25** | twenty-five | **200** | two hundred |
| **12** | twelve | **26** | twenty-six | **212** | two hundred and twelve |
| **13** | thirteen | **27** | twenty-seven | **1000** | one thousand |
| **14** | fourteen | **28** | twenty-eight | **4,354** | four thousand, three hundred and fifty-four |

## 5 Numbers

Listen to the CD and write down the numbers, times and prices you hear.

## 6 What is it?

Match the words to the pictures.

oranges ◆ apples ◆ bananas ◆ tomatoes ◆ pretzel ◆ carrots
sandwich ◆ muffin ◆ doughnut ◆ eggs ◆ orange juice
mineral water ◆ milk ◆ newspaper

## 7 Have you got ...?

In pairs, ask your partner if she or he has got the things in the photos on page 15 and ask for the price.

START LIKE THIS **A** Excuse me, have you got any oranges?
**B** Yes, we have.
**A** How much are they?
**B** They are 88 pence a kilo.

## 8 On the checkout

Put the shop assistant's sentences in the correct places. Then read the dialogue.

That's €10.50 please.

I think I can manage. Here's your change and your receipt.

That's no problem. Have you got 50 cents?

Thank you. Goodbye.

Have you got a 50 cent coin?

SHOP ASSISTANT ...1
CUSTOMER I'm sorry, I've only got a €100 note.
SHOP ASSISTANT ...2
CUSTOMER Pardon?
SHOP ASSISTANT ...3
CUSTOMER No, sorry, I haven't.
SHOP ASSISTANT ...4
CUSTOMER Thank you.
SHOP ASSISTANT ...5

**BEING POLITE**

| | |
|---|---|
| sorry | *Entschuldigen Sie. (tut mir Leid)* |
| excuse me | *Entschuldigen Sie (können Sie mir bitte sagen, ...)* |
| please | *Bitte (ich möchte etwas ...)* |
| here you are | *Bitte (hier bitte / hier ist es / hier haben Sie es)* |
| you're welcome | *Bitte (gern geschehen / Antwort auf danke)* |
| pardon? | *Bitte? (ich habe Sie nicht verstanden)* |

## 9 Dialogue

Work with a partner to make a dialogue in English. Then practise it with other items (such as oranges, apples, etc.).

| **Customer** | **Shop assistant** |
|---|---|
| Fragen Sie, ob er/sie Bananen hat. | |
| | Sagen Sie, dass sie welche haben. |
| Fragen Sie nach dem Preis. | |
| | Sagen Sie den Preis je Kilogramm. Fragen Sie, wie viele er/sie möchte. |
| Sagen Sie, Sie möchten sieben Bananen. | |
| | Sie haben nicht richtig verstanden und fragen noch einmal nach. |
| Sagen Sie noch einmal die Menge. | |
| | Geben Sie ihm/ihr die Bananen und fragen Sie, ob er/sie noch etwas möchte. |
| Sagen Sie, nein, danke, das ist alles. | |
| | Sagen Sie den Preis (2,05 Euro) |
| Geben Sie einen 50 Euro-Schein. | |
| | Fragen Sie, ob er/sie 5 Cent hat. |
| Geben Sie ihm/ihr 5 Cent. | |
| | Geben Sie ihm/ihr das Wechselgeld und den Kassenbon. |

## 10 Role play

Student A (customer) look below; student B (shop assistant) look at File 3 on page 93. You are both at a grocery shop.

**CUSTOMER**

You would like to buy the things on the list. Ask the shop assistant if she or he has got them and ask for the price.

| | |
|---|---|
| *orange juice 1 bottle* | *doughnuts 2* |
| *pretzels 2* | *sandwiches 4* |
| *oranges 2 kilograms* | *milk 1 litre* |
| *apples 1 kilogram* | *bananas 5* |
| *apple juice 1 bottle* | *muffins 2* |
| *German newspaper 1* | *cucumbers 3* |

UNIT

# 3 At the supermarket

## 1 Where is it?

Choose the correct words to complete the sentences.

straight ahead ◆ on the left
on the right ◆ in the corner
in the first aisle ◆ in the last aisle
in the second aisle
in the third aisle ◆ round
behind ◆ between ◆ in front of
near ◆ next to ◆ opposite

*1* Fruit and vegetables are ... ... .
*2* Pasta and flour are ... .
*3* Vegetables are ... the fruit.
*4* The deli counter is ... .
*5* Ask the shop assistant ... the deli counter.
*6* There's a trolley ... the deli counter.
*7* Jam is just ... the corner.
*8* Soft drinks are ... .
*9* The dairy products are ... .
*10* Sausages are ... .
*11* Pet food is ... the washing powder.
*12* Spices are ... the frozen food and the eggs.
*13* The checkouts are ... the exit.
*14* Shampoo is ... .

### ASKING FOR THINGS IN A SHOP

| | |
|---|---|
| Excuse me, could you tell me where I can find ...? | Certainly, sir/madam. |
| Excuse me, where is ...? | Go straight on / straight ahead. |
| Excuse me, where are ...? | It's in the first aisle on the left/on the right. |
| Could you help me please? I can't find ... | They are in the last aisle, next to .... |
| | Turn round the corner into the next aisle. |
| | They're over there, next to ... |
| Thanks a lot. | |
| Thank you very much. | You're welcome. |

## 2 Getting help

Emily is in the first aisle, at the shelf with the sugar. Read or listen to the dialogues and, in pairs, make up similar ones.

CUSTOMER 1 Excuse me, could you help me? I can't find the spices.
EMILY Certainly sir, go round the corner and straight on. They're on the left, next to the frozen food.
CUSTOMER 1 Thank you very much.
EMILY You're welcome.

CUSTOMER 2 Excuse me, where is the cat food?
EMILY Over there, madam, in the third aisle, in the corner.
CUSTOMER 2 Thanks a lot.
EMILY You're welcome.

GRAMMAR CHECK

### PRONOUNS

*1* Excuse me. That trolley belongs to **me**.
*2* No, I'm sorry. It's **my** trolley.
*3* No, I'm afraid you're wrong. It's **mine**.
*4* You're both wrong. I put these things in the trolley **myself**, so it's mine.

- *Im Englischen gibt es für jede Person eine Objektform der Personalpronomen, z. B. steht* me *für mich bzw. mir (1).* My, your, her *usw. steht vor einem Hauptwort (2),* mine, yours, hers *usw. steht alleine, d. h. ohne Hauptwort (3). Reflexivpronomen heben hervor, dass etwas selbst – ohne fremde Hilfe – getan wurde (4).*

| **personal pronouns (object)** | **possessive adjectives** | **possessive pronouns** | **reflexive pronouns** |
|---|---|---|---|
| me | my | mine | myself |
| you | your | yours | yourself |
| him | his | his | himself |
| her | her | hers | herself |
| it | its | — | itself |
| us | our | ours | ourselves |
| you | your | yours | yourselves |
| them | their | theirs | themselves |

## 3 Practice

Rewrite the sentences.

EXAMPLE This is my book. *It's mine. It belongs to me.*

*1* This is Emily's money.
*2* It's our car.
*3* This is your shopping bag.
*4* Are these Harry's biscuits?
*5* Is this Keith and Miriam's house?
*6* These are my apples.

## 4 Practice

Complete the sentences with the correct pronouns.

EXAMPLE This is ... (he) shopping bag. *This is **his** shopping bag.*

*1* Is that your trolley? No, it's ... (she).
*2* Could you give ... (I) 20 grams of ham, please?
*3* What is this street called? I don't know ... (it) name.
*4* Is that money ... (you)?
*5* Could you give ... (he) the apples, please?
*6* Could you tell ... (we) where the biscuits are?
*7* I don't like ... (they).
*8* She doesn't like ... (he) very much.
*9* They really love ... (she).
*10* Is that ... (we) car over there?

## 5 Practice

Complete the sentences.

EXAMPLE Emily is making the cake … . *Emily is making the cake* ***herself***.

1 Emily and Daniel do not need help, they can do it … .
2 The machine cleans … .
3 If I want to save money, I have to do it … .
4 Tim, can you do it … or shall I help you?
5 Hannah is cleaning the windows … .
6 I can type the letter …, I don't need any help.
7 We don't need your help, we can do it … .
8 Harry can't fix the car …, he must take it to a garage.
9 Emily and Jeremy, can you do it … or do you need help?
10 Jason, did you eat all those sandwiches … ?

**ORDINAL NUMBERS**

| | | | | | |
|---|---|---|---|---|---|
| **1st** | first | **11th** | eleventh | **21st** | twenty-first |
| **2nd** | second | **12th** | twelfth | **22nd** | twenty-second |
| **3rd** | third | **13th** | thirteenth | **23rd** | twenty-third |
| **4th** | fourth | **14th** | fourteenth | **24th** | twenty-fourth |
| **5th** | fifth | **15th** | fifteenth | **25th** | twenty-fifth |
| **6th** | sixth | **16th** | sixteenth | **30th** | thirtieth |
| **7th** | seventh | **17th** | seventeenth | **40th** | fortieth |
| **8th** | eighth | **18th** | eighteenth | **50th** | fiftieth |
| **9th** | ninth | **19th** | nineteenth | **78th** | seventy-eighth |
| **10th** | tenth | **20th** | twentieth | **100th** | hundredth |

## 6 Listening

Listen to the CD and write down the words in the correct order.

aisle ◆ birthday ◆ bottle
customer ◆ day ◆ job ◆ month
shelf ◆ street ◆ tin ◆ trolley
week ◆ year

## 7 Items in a supermarket

Match the pictures with the words below.

bacon ◆ beans ◆ beer ◆ butter ◆ cauliflower ◆ cheese
chicken ◆ lobster ◆ mineral water (still or fizzy) ◆ nutmeg
parsley ◆ pineapple ◆ sardines ◆ soap ◆ strawberries
toilet paper ◆ washing powder ◆ washing-up liquid

## 8

Draw a word spider like the one below and complete it with the words above. Use a dictionary to add some more words.

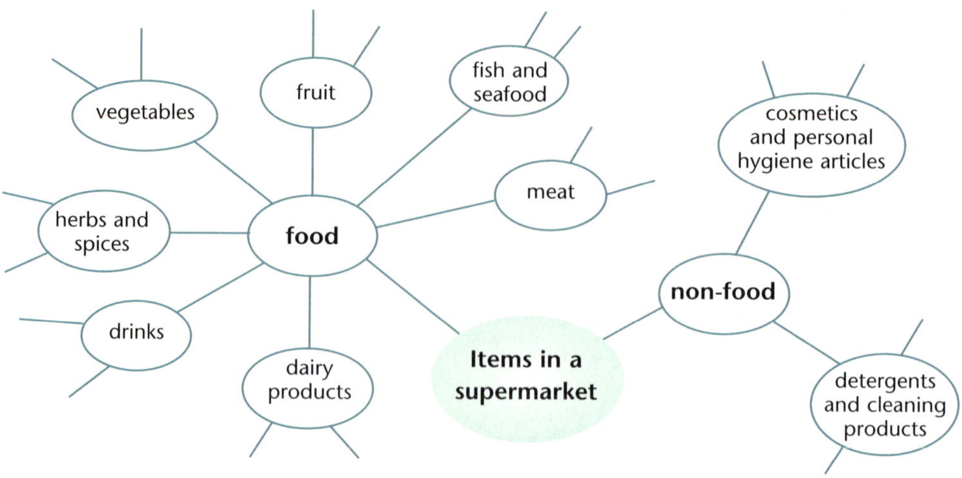

## 9 A shopping list

Sometimes customers can't come to the supermarket so they ask SNIPS to deliver to their homes. One day, Emily is in the office when a customer calls. Emily takes the customer's order but makes some mistakes. Listen to the dialogue and correct her mistakes.

START LIKE THIS Mr Hammon doesn't want six tomatoes, he wants six tins of tomatoes.

**George Hammon, 24 Southwood Avenue**

- 6 tomatoes
- 3 tins of beans
- 2 chickens (fresh)
- 10 bottles of apple juice
- 3 apples
- 2 packets of washing powder
- 13 bottles of mineral water (fizzy)
- 1 large packet of nuts
- 5 chocolate muffins

## 10 Egg do's and don'ts

Read the information about Lion Quality Eggs and tell someone who doesn't speak English what it means. Why is it important to be careful with eggs?

### Egg Do's and Don'ts

- **Do** buy eggs with the Lion Quality mark on the box
- **Do** store eggs in the fridge
- **Do** eat eggs by the best-before date
- **Do** wash hands before and after handling eggs
- **Don't** eat cracked or dirty eggs
- **Don't** eat raw eggs
- **Don't** eat lightly cooked eggs if you are pregnant or in a vulnerable group

UNIT

# 4 A letter from Emily

Dear Monika,

Hello, my name is Emily Jones. I'm answering your ad in "Hello" magazine and I'd like to exchange letters with you. Let me tell you something about myself. I'm 17 years old and I live with my mother and my brother Daniel – he is 15 – in a little house in London. My mother is a nurse at St. Anne's hospital, and my brother still goes to school. My father is an office clerk, but I don't see him very often, because my parents are divorced.

We've also got a cat. His name is Terence and he's a three-year old grey and white tabby. Have you got a pet?

I'm a trainee at a supermarket near here. I like the work but I don't like the hours. Sometimes I have to start at 8 am and work till 5 pm and sometimes I can start later but I have to work until 8 pm. Twice a week I've got an afternoon off. Every three weeks I have to work on Saturdays.

In my spare time I like playing tennis and I like going to the cinema. What do you do in your spare time? What kind of music do you like? Who's your favourite pop star or group?

I can speak a little French but I don't know any German, so please write to me in English. I'm looking forward to your letters.

Best wishes,
Emily

**My name is Monika.** I'd like to have pen-friends all over the world. Please write in German or English to Monika Gartner, Neubaugasse 4, 1070 Vienna, Austria.

**Hello, my name is Istvan.** I'm 17 and I'd like to write to pen-friends all over the world. My hobbies are playing the guitar and computer games. Please write in Hungarian or English to Istvan Horvath, Erzsebet utca 25, Sopron, Hungary.

**Hi, I'm 18, a student**, and I'm looking for pen-friends in Europe or the USA. My hobbies are sailing, cycling, and music (I'm a singer in a band). Please write in German or English to Henning Schmitt, Nissenstr. 31, 22149 Hamburg, Germany.

**Who wants to write me?** My name is Vanessa, I'm 16 and I'm still at school. I love the music of the fifties and sixties. Please write in English to Vanessa Roberts, 34, Penny Lane, Liverpool, Great Britain.

**I'm looking for male and female pen-friends** from Italian or English speaking countries. My hobbies are skiing and surfing. I'm a trainee car mechanic and I like motorbikes. Please write to Antonia Rosso, Via Ernesto Codignola 65, Florence, Italy.

**Hi! I'm Erkan** and I'm 17 years old. I would like to exchange letters with girls from all over Europe. I speak English, German and Turkish, but my English is better than my German. I like travelling and animals. Please write to Erkan Yilmaz, Ankara Caddesi 95, Istanbul, Turkey.

**1** Read the letter and say if the sentences below are true or false.

1. Emily wants to exchange letters with Monika.
2. Her brother works in an office.
3. Her parents are divorced.
4. Her cat is female.
5. She works at a supermarket.
6. She has to work from 8 am to 8 pm.
7. She sometimes has to work on Saturdays.
8. Every two weeks she's got an afternoon off.
9. She doesn't like tennis.
10. She doesn't know any French.

## TELLING THE TIME

*Bei Angabe von Minuten, die nicht durch 5 teilbar sind, muss man das Wort* minutes *hinzufügen, z. B.* six minutes past one, eleven minutes to two.

*Das Wort* o'clock *wird nur mit der vollen Stunde verwendet.*
*Außer bei Fahrplänen ist die Angabe 13 Uhr, 14 Uhr usw. im Englischen nicht üblich.*

2.00 = two (o'clock) in the morning *oder* two am
14.30 = half past two in the afternoon or two thirty pm
19.15 = (a) quarter past seven in the evening *oder* seven fifteen pm
23.45 = (a) quarter to twelve at night *oder* eleven forty-five pm

| | |
|---|---|
| in the morning | *am Morgen* |
| in the afternoon | *am Nachmittag* |
| in the evening | *am Abend* |
| at night | *in der Nacht* |
| from seven thirty am until 6 pm | *von 7.30 bis 18.00 Uhr* |
| nearly 6 (o'clock) am | *beinahe 6.00 (Uhr)* |
| just after 3 (o'clock) pm | *kurz nach 15.00 Uhr* |
| around 5 (o'clock) am | *gegen 5 Uhr, etwa 5 Uhr* |
| today | *heute* |
| tonight | *heute Abend/Nacht* |
| yesterday | *gestern* |
| tomorrow | *morgen* |

## 2 Emily's day

Match the sentences with the pictures.

*1*

*5*

*2*

*6*

*3*

*7*

*4*

*8*

She gets to work at two minutes to eight.

She leaves the supermarket at ten past five.

Emily gets up at ten to seven.

She gets home at twenty-five past five.

She catches the bus at a quarter to eight.

She has breakfast at twenty past seven.

She finishes work at five.

She has her lunch break from half past twelve to half past one

## 3 What time is it?

Write down the time as shown in the example. Use am / pm.

*1* 

*It's five twenty am.*

*2* 

*3* 

*4* 

*5* 

*6* 

*7* 

*8* 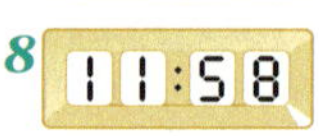


*9* 

*10* 

## 4 Harry's morning shift

Listen to Harry talk about his day and write down the times you hear. Listen again and take notes about Harry's working day.

START LIKE THIS Harry's alarm clock rings at …

## 5 Daily routine

Find the matching answers for the questions.

1 When do you get up on weekdays?
2 And on Sundays?
3 When you go to work, what time do you leave home?
4 How do you get to work?
5 How long does that take?
6 When do you have lunch?
7 How long is your lunch break?
8 What time do you finish work?

a One hour.
b Most days I finish at 6, but sometimes I have to work later or sometimes I can go home earlier.
c Some time between 12 and 1.
d I usually leave just after half past seven.
e About twenty minutes.
f I have to get up at twenty to seven.
g First I go on the underground and then I take the bus.
h I usually get up at around 10 o'clock.

## 6 Practice

Find the right word order and rewrite the sentences.

*1* does / time / the / leave / next / bus / What?
*2* leaves / next / bus / at / The / 9.25.
*3* does / time / in / your / shop / morning / open / the / What?
*4* opens / shop / 9 / at / Our / past / half.
*5* Friday / to / at / we / 6.30 / close / From / Monday.
*6* Saturdays / open / On / 5.00 / are / we / until.

GRAMMAR CHECK

### HAVE (GOT) TO / WOULD LIKE TO

**have (got) to** *(müssen)*

*1* I **have to** / I'**ve got to** work until 8 pm.
*2* Harry **doesn't have to** / **hasn't got to** work tomorrow.
*3* **Does** Emily **have to** / **Has** Emily **got to** work tomorrow?

- Have (got) to *drückt eine Notwendigkeit bzw Verpflichtung aus.* *Verneinung* = don't have to *bzw.* haven't got to *(nicht müssen, nicht brauchen).* *Die Formen sind dieselben wie für* have/have got *(siehe Seite 13).*

**would like to** *(möchte, hätte gerne)*

*1* I'**d** (= I would) **like to** have pen-friends all over the world.
*2* She **wouldn't like to** write in French.
*3* **Would** you **like to** learn French?

- Would like to *drückt einen Wunsch aus. Die Formen sind für alle Personen gleich; die Kurzform lautet* 'd (I'd, you'd, she'd like to *usw.*).

⚠ I **like** this book. *Mir gefällt dieses Buch.*
I **like** reading books. *Ich lese gern.*
I'**d like** this book. *Ich möchte dieses Buch haben.*

## 7 Practice

Complete the sentences with words from the box.

| |
|---|
| like ◆ likes ◆ would like ◆ would like ◆ would not like<br>have to ◆ has to |

*1* I ... go now, I'm afraid. It's very late.
*2* I ... going out with friends.
*3* Harry ... to sleep until 11 am tomorrow but ... get up early.
*4* Emily ... her cat very much.
*5* Do you think your sister ... that pink T-shirt?
*6* I'm certain that she ... it. She hates pink.

## 8 Translation

Translate these sentences into German. Then close the book and translate them back into English. Check with the original sentences.

*1* I like to get up late on Sundays.
*2* I'd like to get up late every morning, but I have to go to work.
*3* I like writing letters to my pen-friend.
*4* I'd like to meet my pen-friend one day.
*5* I've got a cat and I like him very much.
*6* I'd like to have more time to play with my cat.
*7* I don't like dogs very much.
*8* I'd like to have two days off next week.

## 9 Practice

Complete the sentences with the correct form of the verb. Then think of some more things you and your friends like or don't like.

*1* In my spare time I ... (like) reading.
*2* Emily ... (like) her job but she ... (not/like) the hours.
*3* My brother ... (like) his hamster very much.
*4* I ... (like) cats but I ... (not/like) dogs.
*5* All young people ... (like) listening to music.
*6* My pen-friend ... (like) skiing, but she ... (not/like) tennis.
*7* Some of my friends say they ... (like) their work.
*8* Sheila says she ... (not/like) her work.

## ADVERBS OF FREQUENCY *(Häufigkeitsadverbien)*

| | | | |
|---|---|---|---|
| always | *immer* | sometimes | *manchmal* |
| usually | *normalerweise* | hardly ever | *kaum* |
| normally | *normalerweise* | never | *niemals* |
| often | *oft* | | |

## TIME PHRASES *(adverbiale Bestimmungen der Zeit)*

| | |
|---|---|
| once | an hour |
| twice | a day |
| three times | a week / a month |
| several times | a year |
| in the | morning / afternoon |
| every | Friday / month / two weeks |

⚠ *Achten Sie auf die Satzstellung:*

**Sometimes** I have to start work at 8 am.
I **usually** drink coffee before work.
I drink coffee **in the morning**.

## 10 Do you sometimes ...?

Make sentences using the words below and the frequency adverbs and time phrases from the box above.

*1* drink coffee in the morning
*2* get up before 6 o'clock
*3* go to bed after 11 o'clock
*4* leave home without breakfast
*5* play tennis
*6* go swimming
*7* go to the cinema
*8* buy a doughnut
*9* speak English

## 11 Practice

Complete the sentences with the words below.

after ◆ early ◆ late ◆ before ◆ in ◆ at ◆ nearly ◆ from ◆ until

*1* Tomorrow I have to get up very ..., I've got to work a morning shift.
*2* I have to go now, it's very ....
*3* Aren't you hungry? It's ... lunch-time.
*4* The bread is delivered ... I start work.
*5* Do you sometimes have to work ... the evening?
*6* I work ... 8 o'clock in the morning ... 5 o'clock in the evening.
*7* My mother is a nurse, she sometimes works ... night.
*8* ... lunch I always have a cup of coffee.

## 12 Yes or no?

Work with a partner. Student A look below and student B look at File 5 on page 94.

**A**

Your partner has some information about Emily's cousin Kevin Davies. Try to find out as much as possible about Kevin, but your partner can only answer "yes" or "no".

*1* How old is he?
*2* When does he get up?
*3* Does he work or does he go to school?
*4* How long does it take him to get there?
*5* Which animals does he like?
*6* What does he like to do in his spare time?
*7* Which sport does he play in his spare time?
*8* Which English city does he live in?
*9* What about his family?

Can you think of some more questions?

## 13 A letter

Look again at the advertisements on page 24 and reply to one of them. Write about yourself.

## 14 Puzzle

Find 3 seasons, 5 days of the week and 11 months in the puzzle. Write the words on a separate piece of paper. What words are missing?

| | | | | | | | | | | | |
|---|---|---|---|---|---|---|---|---|---|---|---|
| R | F | R | I | D | A | Y | Q | R | R | N | K |
| X | E | H | R | P | V | A | C | E | E | D | K |
| R | H | B | R | Q | Y | A | M | B | T | X | H |
| B | E | I | M | A | U | T | U | M | N | J | I |
| A | L | B | D | E | S | P | T | E | I | A | E |
| U | U | N | O | U | V | U | M | T | W | N | H |
| U | U | G | M | T | I | O | O | P | M | U | C |
| S | I | M | U | N | C | R | N | E | V | A | R |
| R | E | Z | E | S | W | O | D | S | W | R | A |
| R | H | N | D | B | T | I | A | U | K | Y | M |
| T | U | E | S | D | A | Y | Y | B | M | R | X |
| J | E | R | F | E | B | R | U | A | R | Y | G |
| J | U | L | Y | Y | A | D | S | R | U | H | T |

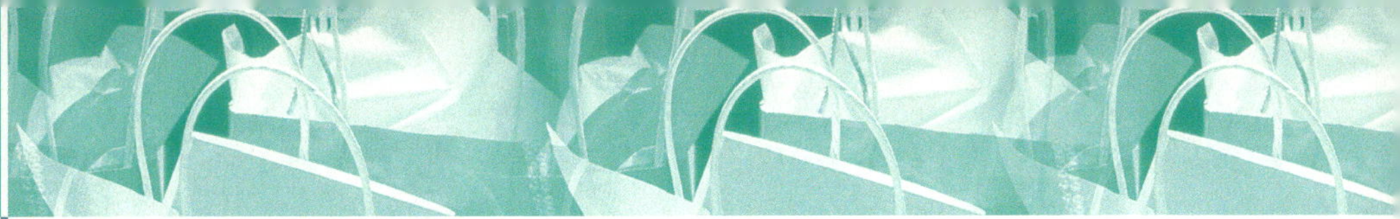

# UNIT 5 | *The ideal shopper*

## 1 What kind of shopper are you?

Answer the questions and then look at the types of shoppers below. Can you identify yourself? Work with a partner and find out what kind of shopper he or she is.

Do you ... only buy the things on your shopping list?
... write shopping lists, but also buy other goods?
... never write a shopping list?
... look for special offers?
... usually only buy things you already know?
... like to try out new things?
... have a household budget?
... usually buy healthy food like organically grown vegetables and free-range eggs?
... sometimes buy things you don't need?
... never have much time for shopping?
... usually compare prices in different shops?

**Mr and Mrs Sensible** write a shopping list at home but also make decisions when they are in the shop. They look for special offers and buy things that are reduced in price (for example fruit or vegetables at the end of the day). They are also very careful. For example, they look at the dates on food packages.

**Mr and Mrs Habit** like routines. They know exactly what they want and buy just that. They plan their meals and often cook and buy the same things.

**Mr and Mrs Green** are idealists who like organic food and environmentally friendly products. They try to buy products without too much packaging. They often have strange things on their shopping lists and they ask a lot of questions.

**Mr and Mrs Hectic** have no time to shop. They often have a busy job and often also have young children. They shop quickly and like to know where everything is in the shop.

**Mr and Mrs Impulse** have no shopping list and no household budget. They often buy new things "because they look nice" even if they don't really need them.

## 2 Types of shoppers

Now work with a partner and answer these questions. Do you agree or disagree with your partner? Give your opinion.

*1* Which kind of shoppers do supermarkets like? Why?
*2* Which kind of shoppers do they not like very much? Why?
*3* Which kind of shoppers seem to enjoy shopping and which probably hate it? Why?

### GIVING AN OPINION

I think / I believe / I feel (that) …
In my opinion, supermarkets like … but they don't like …

### AGREEING AND DISAGREEING

I agree. I think so, too.
No, I'm sorry. I don't agree.
I disagree with you. I think …

GRAMMAR CHECK

### ADVERBS

*1* I **usually** only buy the things on my shopping list.
*2* You are **terribly** late.
*3* He works very **hard**.

- *Das Adverb bezieht sich meist auf ein Verb (1) oder auf ein Adjektiv (2). Die meisten Adverbien werden durch das Anhängen von* -ly *an das Adjektiv gebildet (1, 2).*

⚠ *Beachten Sie einige Ausnahmen:*

| *Adjektiv* | *Adverb* |
|---|---|
| good | well |
| fast | fast |
| hard | hard (3) (hardly = *kaum*) |
| late | late (lately = *neulich*) |
| near | near (nearly = *fast*) |

## 3 Practice

Complete the sentences with adverbs from the box.

| |
|---|
| badly ◆ certainly ◆ completely ◆ directly ◆ environmentally organically ◆ probably ◆ properly ◆ quickly ◆ well |

*1* We also sell … grown fruit and vegetables.
*2* Deborah lives in Germany and speaks German quite … .
*3* This product line is … friendly – it has very little packaging.
*4* You can … go home early today. I'm not 100% certain but we're not very busy.
*5* Emily works fast, so I think she can finish this work very … .
*6* Mrs Wood is waiting for this letter. Could you take it to her …, please?
*7* Have we got any toothpaste? The shelf is … empty.
*8* Please don't use that box. It's … damaged.
*9* Mrs Wood knows everything, she can … help you.
*10* Don't use that calculator. It doesn't work … .

## 4 Adverb or adjective?

Choose the correct word in each sentence.

*1* She is a very *sensible/sensibly* shopper.
*2* They *near/nearly* always buy the same things.
*3* I know *exact/exactly* what I want.
*4* This is not the *exact/exactly* time.
*5* Mr and Mrs Sensible are *slow/slowly* shoppers.
*6* They take their time and shop *slow/slowly*.
*7* Be *careful/carefully* on your way home!
*8* Some supermarkets watch their customers *careful/carefully*.
*9* Mrs Hectic shops very *quick/quickly*, she is always *short/shortly* of time.

## 5 What is she doing?

Emily is in the office at SNIPS. She is sitting by a monitor and is watching the shoppers. What is Mrs Anderson doing? Match the sentences to the pictures.

Now she's taking a tin of cat food and is putting it into her trolley.

She's looking at a jar of jam. But she isn't taking it, she's putting it back.

She's taking a trolley.

She's leaving the shop.

She's looking at her shopping list.

She's entering the shop.

She's paying at the checkout.

GRAMMAR CHECK

### PRESENT CONTINUOUS (-ing form)

*1* She**'s** (= She is) entering the shop.
*2* What**'s** (= What is) she doing now?
*3* She **isn't** (= is not) taking the jam.

- *Die Verlaufsform der Gegenwart* (-ing-*Form) drückt aus, dass ein Vorgang zeitgleich mit dem Sprechen stattfindet. Diese Form wird gebildet mit dem Verb* be + *der* ing-*Form des Vollverbs (1–3).*

| Statements | Questions | Negatives |
|---|---|---|
| I am working | am I working? | I am not working |
| you are working | are you working? | you are not working |
| he/she/it is working | is he/she/it working? | he/she/it is not working |
| we are working | are we working? | we are not working |
| you are working | are you working? | you are not working |
| they are working | are they working? | they are not working |

**Short answers**

Yes, he is. No, she isn't.
Yes, I am. No, I'm not.

## 6 Practice

Complete the sentences with the present continuous form of the verb.

*1* I … (do) my shopping.
*2* … (you/come) with me?
*3* He … (wait) for his wife.
*4* She … (drive) her car.
*5* It … (not/work) properly.
*6* We … (look) for fresh vegetables.
*7* How … (you/pay)?
*8* They … (pay) cash.

## 7 Practice

Simple present or present continuous? Complete the sentences with the correct form of the verb.

*1* He … (not/live) with his parents. He … (have got) his own flat.
*2* Now he is on holiday in France. He … (shop) in a supermarket.
*3* Harry is a shop assistant. He … (work) at SNIPS supermarket.
*4* Usually he … (not/work) on the checkout, he … (sell) cheese.
*5* But today two cashiers … (have) a day off, so he … (work) on the checkout.
*6* Rhaina … (not/go) to work this morning. She … (take) her little brother to the hospital.
*7* Fiona and Sally are cashiers. They … (not/work) at the deli counter.
*8* They … (take) money from the customers and … (give) them their change.
*9* Look at Sally! What … (she/do) now?
*10* She … (give) a receipt to a customer.
*11* Emily always … (leave) the house at 7.40 am.
*12* She usually … (catch) the bus at a quarter to eight.

## 8 The shoplifter

What is happening here? Describe the story in your own words.

## 9 How to stop shoplifters

SNIPS has a problem with shoplifters. One day, Mrs Woods asks everybody for their ideas on how to stop people from stealing. Listen to their ideas and match them to the pictures. Which idea(s) do you agree with?

## 10 Puzzle

Find ten words in the puzzle to fill the gaps in the table below. Translate all the words and use three of them in sentences.

| | | | | | | | | | | |
|---|---|---|---|---|---|---|---|---|---|---|
| E | P | A | C | K | E | T | M | E | N | T |
| D | E | A | S | I | T | Y | U | C | N | O |
| E | N | T | R | A | N | C | E | O | S | P |
| L | E | G | A | M | A | D | E | O | R | A |
| I | A | V | O | U | R | D | L | K | E | C |
| V | P | A | R | R | I | V | A | L | I | K |
| E | E | D | U | C | T | I | O | N | H | A |
| R | T | N | E | M | Y | A | P | Z | S | G |
| Y | O | D | C | H | A | N | G | E | A | I |
| D | I | S | E | Z | T | I | O | N | C | N |
| C | A | L | C | U | L | A | T | O | R | G |

| verb | noun |
|---|---|
| arrive | ...1 |
| calculate | ...2 |
| ...3 | cook |
| ...4 | decision |
| enter | ...5 |
| ...6 | change |
| pack | ...7, ...8 |
| cash | cash, ...9 |
| deliver | ...10 |

UNIT

# 6 Shopping in Main Street

## 1 Shopping in Main Street

Look at the different types of shops. What do you think you can buy there?

## 2 Listening

Listen to the four dialogues. Where do you think the people are? Match the dialogues to the shops above.

## 3 Things you can buy

Match the words to the pictures.

half a dozen pork sausages

a bar of chocolate

a bottle of contact lens cleaner

a lighter

a bunch of grapes

a bunch of roses

an English/German dictionary

an iron

a head of lettuce

a jar of jam

a loaf of wholemeal bread

a packet of painkillers

a pair of silver earrings

a pair of sunglasses

a pair of tights

a tube of glue

tennis balls

a tin of shoe polish

a tub of margarine

a tube of toothpaste

## 4 Where will you go first?

Look at the above list and plan your shopping tour through Main Street.

START LIKE THIS First, I'll go to the shoe shop and buy a tin of shoe polish. Then I'll go …

**SEQUENCE WORDS**

First, … Then, … Next, … After that, … Finally, …

GRAMMAR CHECK

### EXPRESSING THE FUTURE (1)

*1* I'**ll** (= I **will**) **take** that bunch there.
*2* First I'**ll go** to the shoe shop.
*3* Where **will** you **go** first?

- *Das* will-future *wird gebildet mit* will + *Infinitiv des Vollverbs. Es hat für alle Personen die gleiche Form.*
- *Das Futur mit* will *(= werden) wird unter anderem für spontane Entscheidungen verwendet (1–3). Andere Verwendungsmöglichkeiten stehen auf Seite 45.*

## 5 Practice

Match the sentences on the left to the responses.

1 Would you like this dictionary or that one?
2 Oh dear, we haven't got any flour.
3 What would you like to drink?
4 How many apples would you like?
5 Henry, can you start work at 7 am tomorrow?
6 Emily, where's Rhaina?

I'll take one kilo, please.
Yes, no problem. I'll catch the early bus.
I'll buy some tomorrow.
I don't know but I'll find her for you.
I'll take this one.
I'll have a cola, please.

### COUNTABLE AND UNCOUNTABLE NOUNS AND PAIR WORDS

| **countable** *(zählbar)* | **uncountable** *(nicht zählbar)* | **pair words** *(Paarwörter)* |
|---|---|---|
| (a) few oranges<br>*wenige Orangen* | a little coffee<br>*ein bisschen Kaffee* | some tights<br>*eine Strumpfhose* |
| some peanuts<br>*ein paar Erdnüsse* | some sugar<br>*etwas Zucker* | a pair of glasses<br>*eine Brille* |
| several = a couple of customers<br>*einige Kunden* | a lot of (= much) milk<br>*eine Menge (= viel) Milch* | two pairs of trousers<br>*zwei (Paar) Hosen* |
| a lot of (= many) people<br>*eine Menge (= viele) Leute* | | |

## 6 Translation

Translate the following expressions into German. Then close the book and translate them back into English. Check with the original words.

*1* A lot of margarine
*2* A little mustard
*3* Some wholemeal bread
*4* Some bananas
*5* A pair of tights
*6* A pair of sunglasses
*7* A few slices of ham
*8* Several pieces of cake
*9* Some vinegar
*10* A little lemon juice
*11* Many bars of chocolate
*12* A lot of shoe polish
*13* There are only a few people in the shop.
*14* There is very little work today.
*15* There is a lot to do.
*16* There are several customers waiting.

## 7 At a bakery

CUSTOMER Good morning. Um – excuse me, my German is very poor, I'm afraid. Do you speak English?

SALES Yes, a little. What would you like?

CUSTOMER Well, I'd like some bread, but you've got such a variety that I don't know which to choose. Could you help me a bit?

SALES Do you prefer white bread or brown bread?

CUSTOMER Brown bread, but not too brown.

SALES Now, this one here is rye bread. I don't think you'd like that very much, it's very dark. But those ones over there are different kinds of wholemeal bread, mainly made of wheat, but also containing other things. This one here has linseeds and poppy seeds, this one sunflower seeds, this one has pumpkin seeds, and that one over there is olive bread, and the one next to it is walnut bread.

CUSTOMER Oh dear, that all sounds delicious. Could you give me one loaf of sunflower bread and one of those with olives.

SALES Certainly, sir. Would you like anything else?

CUSTOMER Yes, what about these pastries here? What are they filled with?

| | |
|---|---|
| SALES | This one is apple strudel, it's filled with apple and cinnamon. These ones here are filled with vanilla custard. The ones over there are made with different kinds of nuts and the other ones over there are filled with sweet cheese and apricot. |
| CUSTOMER | Mmm ... can I have two pieces of apple strudel and one nut pastry, please? |
| SALES | OK. Anything else? |
| CUSTOMER | No, thanks, that's all. |
| SALES | Would you like a carrier bag? |
| CUSTOMER | No, thank you, I've got a shopping bag. I must say, your English is very good. |
| SALES | Thank you. So, that's €8.25 altogether. |
| CUSTOMER | Here you are. |
| SALES | Your change and your receipt. Thank you very much, sir. Have a nice day. |
| CUSTOMER | Thank you. Goodbye. |

Answer the questions on the dialogue.

1 Which country do you think this bakery is in?
2 Why does the customer not know what to buy?
3 What kind of bread does the customer like?
4 Why would he not like the first kind of bread?
5 What are the wholemeal breads mainly made of?
6 What other things are in them?
7 What kind of bread does the customer buy?
8 What is apple strudel filled with?
9 What are the other pastries made with?
10 What pastries does the customer buy?
11 How much does he pay?
12 Why doesn't he need a carrier bag?

| | | | |
|---|---|---|---|
| this | one | here | *diese/r/s … hier (Einzahl)* |
| these | ones | here | *diese hier (Mehrzahl)* |
| that | one | there | *die/der/das dort (Einzahl)* |
| those | ones | there | *die dort (Mehrzahl)* |

## 8 Practice

Complete the sentences with *this* or *these.*

1 How much is … iron?
2 Are … grapes from Italy?
3 … pastry here looks nice.
4 How much are … matches?
5 I'd like a jar of … honey.
6 I'd like a box of … biscuits.
7 Is … melon fresh?
8 Are … new potatoes?

## 9 Practice

Complete with *this*, *these*, *that* or *those*.

*1* How much is ... tube of toothpaste here?
*2* And how much is ... one over there?
*3* Can you show me ... watch, please? I can't see it from here.
*4* Please give me one jar of ... apricot jam over there and two bags of ... biscuits here.
*5* Which olives do you mean? ... green ones here or ... black ones there?
*6* How much are ... pot plants over there?
*7* So, I'll take ... tennis racket here and two pairs of ... socks over there.
*8* Would you like to try some of ... sausages here?

**GRAMMAR CHECK**

### SOME / ANY

*1* I would like **some** tea and **some** oranges, please.
*2* There aren't **any** people in the shop.
*3* I don't want **any** coffee.
*4* Are there **any** biscuits in the house?
*5* Would you like **some** more tea?
*6* Would you like **anything** else?

- Some *und* any *werden für unbestimmte Mengenangaben – sowohl bei zählbaren Dingen in der Mehrzahl* (some oranges, any people) *als auch bei nicht zählbaren Hauptwörtern* (some tea, any coffee) *– verwendet.*
- Some *steht in bejahten Sätzen (1),* any *steht in Frage- und verneinten Sätzen (2–4).*
- *Wenn auf eine Frage die Antwort „Ja" erwartet wird (höfliches Angebot oder Bitte) wird* some *verwendet (5).*
- some *und* any *können auch mit anderen Wörtern zusammengesetzt werden (6):*

| | | |
|---|---|---|
| something | anything | *etwas* |
| someone / somebody | anyone / anybody | *jemand* |
| somewhere | anywhere | *irgendwo* |

## 10 Practice

Complete the sentences with *some* or *any*.

1 I'd like ... bread, but I don't know which to choose.
2 Would you like ... more biscuits?
3 Is there ...thing else I can do for you?
4 I think there is ...one at the door.
5 Can you see ...one?
6 ...thing strange is going on here.
7 Would you like to try ...thing?
8 I don't need ...thing else, thank you.
9 I really need ... more information on that.
10 We don't have ... apple strudel today.

## 11 Mixed-up dialogue

Put the following dialogue between A (customer) and B (shop assistant) in the correct order.

A Have you got any spinach?

A Excuse me, do you speak English?

A Let's see. I need about half a kilogram. How much is in one packet?

A Thank you. Goodbye.

B Here you are. Your change and your receipt. Thank you.

B Yes, I've got some fresh spinach here and I've also got two kinds of frozen spinach in the freezer.

A Mmm. I'd like frozen spinach, please.

A OK, I'll take two.

B Yes, a little. How can I help you?

B Is there anything else?

B 300 grams. You'll need two packets, then.

B How many packets would you like?

A Here's €3.00.

A No, thanks.

B That'll be €2.90.

## 12 Dialogues

Look again at the picture at the beginning of the unit. Choose three different shops and make up a sales dialogue for each one. Act them out with a partner.

UNIT

# 7 *Eating out*

## 1 At a restaurant

Emily has got a foreign visitor. Her pen-friend Monika is staying with her for a few days. Today they are at a restaurant. Monika speaks English quite well, but she doesn't understand everything on the menu.

EMILY Mmm. This coffee's good. So, do you know what you are going to have, Monika?

MONIKA I'm not sure. I don't understand everything. What are 'sautéed mushrooms'? I know what mushrooms are, but what is 'sautéed'?

EMILY I think it's kind of fried, quickly fried in a very hot pan.

MONIKA I see. And what is a sponge pudding?

EMILY That's a kind of soft, light cake – a traditional English dessert.

MONIKA And cheesecake is made from cheese?

EMILY Not really cheese, it's a cake with sweet, fresh cheese.

MONIKA And what is 'blackberry and apple crumble'? What does 'crumble' mean?

EMILY It has got a crumbly topping of pastry. Do you understand crumbly? Little pieces of pastry.

MONIKA Oh, yes. I think I understand. Maybe I'll try one for dessert. But let's choose a main course first. What is the most traditional English dish?

EMILY That's easy: fish and chips. Do you like fish?

MONIKA Yes, I do. Very much. How is it cooked? What is 'batter'?

EMILY It's a mixture of eggs and flour, I think, and here beer as well. The fillet of fish is first put into the batter and then fried in a pan.

MONIKA All right, that sounds nice. I'll try that. And what about you? Will you have the fish, too?

EMILY No, I won't take the fish today, I think. Um ... let me see.

WAITER May I take your order?

EMILY Yes. I'll have the garlic chicken.

WAITER Would you like vegetables or salad with it?

EMILY A mixed salad and potatoes, please.

WAITER And to drink with your meal?

EMILY A glass of lemonade, please.

MONIKA And I'd like the fish and chips, please, and another cola.

...

WAITER Here are your drinks, ladies. Your meals will be here in a few minutes.

EMILY Thank you.

MONIKA Cheers!

EMILY Cheers!

Answer the questions.

1 What are sautéed mushrooms?
2 What is a sponge pudding?
3 What is a cheesecake?
4 What is blackberry and apple crumble?
5 What are fish and chips?

GRAMMAR CHECK

### EXPRESSING THE FUTURE (2)

1 Your meals **will be** here in a few minutes.
2 I hope you**'ll like** the meal.
3 **Will** you **have** the fish, too?
4 No, I **won't** (= **will** not) **take** the fish today, I think.
5 Monika **is staying** for another four days.

- *Das Futur mit* will *(= werden) verwendet man für zukünftige Situationen oder Ereignisse, die mit Sicherheit eintreten werden (1), für Vermutungen oder Hoffnungen (2) und für spontane Entscheidungen (siehe Seite 39).*
- *Fragen bildet man durch die Veränderung der Satzstellung (3), Verneinungen mit* will not = won't *(4).*
- *Die* -ing-*Form der Gegenwart* (present continuous) *verwendet man, wenn etwas Zukünftiges bereits geplant oder verabredet wurde (5).*

## 2 Practice

Find the right word order and rewrite the sentences. Then translate them into German.

1 ? / dessert / for / have / what / will / you
2 again / go / there / we / won't
3 afraid / I'm / it / like / she / won't
4 ? / another / drink / have / will / you
5 ? / again / back / be / she / when / will
6 have / I / salad / think / I / a / will

## STARTERS

Soup of the Day
*served with fresh bread and butter*
**£2.25**

Chicken Wings
*spicy chicken wings with barbecue sauce*
**£2.45**

Tiger Prawns
*lightly battered with a sweet but hot chilli dip*
**£3.45**

Melon & Forest Fruits
*a slice of melon garnished with forest fruits*
**£2.95**

Duck Paté with Redcurrant Jelly
*served with hot buttered toast*
**£3.45**

## SIDE ORDERS

Onion Rings
**£1.45**

Garlic Bread
**£1.45**

Sautéed Mushrooms
**£1.65**

Portion of Chips
**£1.45**

Bread and Butter
**£1.45**

Side Salad
**£1.65**

## MAIN COURSES

Fish & Chips
*cooked in our own beer batter served with chips*
**£6.25**

Pie of the Day*
*please ask for today's choice*
**£5.25**

Garlic Chicken*
*fried chicken breast with garlic and herb butter*
**£6.45**

Roasted Pepper Lasagne
*red peppers layered with pasta, vegetables and cheese sauce, with garlic bread and a side salad*
**£4.95**

Roast of the Day*
*please ask for today's choice*
**£6.45**

Seafood Pie*
*cod and prawns in a creamy cheese sauce topped with potatoes and cheese*
**£5.75**

Avocado & Sweetcorn Bake
*avocado in a tomato and sweetcorn sauce with cheese and baked golden brown, with garlic bread*
**£6.45**

Coq Au Vin
*chicken in a rich wine sauce, served with white and wild rice and vegetables*
**£7.25**

Sirloin Steak*
*tender sirloin of beef, grilled to your liking*
**£9.25**

**Served with a choice of potatoes and vegetables of the day, or side salad*

## *Speciality of the house*

### *Sausage & Mash*

**Speciality sausages served with mashed potato and onion gravy**

**Please ask for today's sausage choice.**

**£4.95**

## DESSERTS

*All our desserts are served with a choice of cream, ice cream or custard*

Double Chocolate Mousse Cake
**£2.45**

Cheesecake
**£2.75**

Blackberry & Apple Crumble
**£2.45**

Traditional Sponge Pudding
**£2.45**

Cheese & Biscuits
*your choice of cheese served with crispy biscuits – please ask about today's selection of cheeses*
**£3.45**

*All prices include service charge and VAT.*

*The*
# AUSTIN Inn

**BEVERAGES**

Pot of Tea
**95p**

Coffee
**£1.75**

Cappuccino
**£1.75**

Glass of Mineral Water
**95p**

Glass of White or Red Wine
**£1.85**

Glass of Lemonade
**£1.20**

## 3 Taking an order

Work with a partner. Look at the menu and tell your partner what you would like to order. You may use a dictionary for help. Then take the roles of a waitress/waiter and customer and do a role play. The questions below will help you.

**TAKING AN ORDER**

Are you ready to order? / May I take your order?
Would you care for dessert / a starter / some soup / anything to drink?
Would you like vegetables or a salad with that?
How would you like your steak? Rare, medium or well-done?

## 4 What's that in German?

EMILY Your English is great, Monika, I wish I could speak German that well. Can you teach me some? Is it very difficult to learn?

MONIKA It's not very easy, the grammar is quite tricky. But they are related languages. Many words are very similar.

EMILY Really? What for example?

MONIKA 'Soup' is 'Suppe' in German, and 'tomato' is 'Tomate'. So if you want a tomato soup, you ask for a 'Tomatensuppe'.

EMILY 'Tomatensuppe'. That's not very difficult. What else?

MONIKA 'Bread and butter' is 'Brot und Butter'.

EMILY Brot und Butter, Tomatensuppe. That's easy. What is 'garlic' in German?

MONIKA That's 'Knoblauch'.

EMILY Gnob- what? Oh dear. You're right, I'm afraid. It's not very easy.

Continue the conversation of Emily and Monika and find some more words on the menu that are similar in German and English.

**TRUE FRIENDS**

| | |
|---|---|
| tomato | *Tomate* |
| soup | *Suppe* |
| fish | *Fisch* |
| bread | *Brot* |

**FALSE FRIENDS**

| | | | | | |
|---|---|---|---|---|---|
| become | ≠ | *bekommen* | chef | ≠ | *Chef* |
| *werden* | | get | *Küchenchef* | | boss, manager |

*Englisch und Deutsch sind verwandte Sprachen. Manche Wörter sind sehr ähnlich, das sind* true friends, *wie ‚*tomato*' und ‚Tomate'. Es gibt jedoch auch Ausdrücke, die zwar ähnlich klingen, aber eine unterschiedliche Bedeutung haben. Dies sind* false friends, *wie ‚*become*' und ‚bekommen'.*

## 5 True friends and false friends

Find the matching translations. If you need help, work with a partner or use a dictionary.

biscuits, boss, manager, cakes, child, art, custard, dish, coffee, I'm afraid, chef, lettuce, kind, I'm glad, menu, pudding, ring, dish/meal of the day, table, salad, serve, sponge cake, spices, sauce, tablet, tray, water, tea, wine

Art, Biskuit, Chef, ich freue mich, Gewürze, Kaffee, (Blatt) Salat, Salat (z. B. Kartoffelsalat, Nudelsalat), ich befürchte, Kuchen, Kekse, Menü, Tagesteller, Kind, Pudding, Küchenchef, servieren, Soße, Ring, Kunst, Speise, Teller, Speisekarte, Süßspeise, Dessert, Tablett, Tablette (Pille), Tee, Tisch, Wein, Wasser

## 6 What's that in English?

Explain the German menu to someone who doesn't understand German. The following words will help you.

***Types of dishes*** chips ◆ dumplings ◆ salad ◆ soup

***Methods of cooking*** baked ◆ battered ◆ boiled ◆ fried ◆ grilled roast ◆ stewed

***Ingredients*** beef ◆ bread ◆ cabbage ◆ cheese ◆ chicken ◆ garlic leek ◆ lettuce ◆ liver ◆ onion ◆ plaice ◆ pork ◆ potato(es) rice ◆ tomato ◆ veal

***Other useful words*** chops ◆ cream (of) ◆ fillet ◆ French Hungarian ◆ mixed ◆ slice ◆ style

### COOKING TERMS

***cook*** heißt ***Speisen zubereiten***, z. B.

| | | | |
|---|---|---|---|
| bake | *(im Backrohr) backen* | roast | *im Backrohr braten* |
| boil | *kochen, sieden* | sauté | *rösten, rasch anbraten* |
| deep fry | *frittieren* | stew | *dünsten, schmoren* |
| fry | *in einer Pfanne braten* | | |

***Essen*** heißt ***food.***

This restaurant serves traditional **food**. I like Chinese **food** very much.

***Küche*** *(= Art der Zubereitung)* heißt **cuisine**.

I like Indian **cuisine** a lot. French **cuisine** is very famous.

***Küche*** *(Raum in der Speisen zubereitet werden)* heißt **kitchen**.

The **kitchen** is next to the dining room.

⚠ A **cook** *ist ein Koch/eine Köchin aber* **a cooker** *ist ein Herd/ein Kocher.* A **dessert** *ist eine Nachspeise*, a **desert** *ist eine Wüste.*

## 7 Recipe

Below are the instructions for how to cook a traditional German/Austrian dish, but the lines are mixed up. Can you find the correct order? What is the name of the dish?

**WHAT YOU NEED**

2 bread rolls or some white bread

1 egg

a little milk

5 tablespoons of flour

a little salt

fresh parsley

**WHAT YOU DO**

1 sprinkle flour over bread-and-egg-mixture and mix again carefully
2 put bread-cubes in bowl and mix with finely chopped parsley
3 dumplings are done when they start to turn
4 cut white bread or rolls into small cubes (or buy ready-cut bread cubes)
5 mix egg and milk, season with salt
6 put dumplings in boiling water and boil for 5 minutes
7 pour egg-milk mixture over the bread and mix carefully with a spoon
8 form round dumplings with your hands

*Serve as a side dish to roast pork or as a main dish with a creamy mushroom sauce.*

### PLURAL OF NOUNS

**Regular Plural**

| | | | | | |
|---|---|---|---|---|---|
| starter | starters | dessert | desserts | dish | dishes |

**Irregular Plural**

| | | | | | |
|---|---|---|---|---|---|
| *1* | **o** → | **oes** | | | |
| | tomato | tomatoes | but | kilo | kilos |
| | potato | potatoes | | disco | discos |
| *2* | **f/fe** → | **ves** | | | |
| | loaf | loaves | but | safe | safes |
| | shelf | shelves | | roof | roofs |
| | knife | knives | | | |
| *3* | **y** → | **ies** | | | |
| | baby | babies | but | boy | boys |
| | city | cities | | day | days |
| *4* | **other forms** | | | | |
| | foot | feet | | child | children |
| | man | men | | sheep | sheep |
| | woman | women | | fish | fish / fishes |

## 8 Planning a party

Emily is planning a dinner party. Listen to the CD and write down the things she needs. Pay attention to the plural forms of the nouns.

UNIT

# 8 On the telephone

## 1 A message for Emily

Emily's mother, Vera, is at home when the phone rings.

VERA 8613 4257

JILL Hello, Mrs Jones. This is Jill speaking. Can I speak to Emily, please?

VERA Hello, Jill. Emily's not here I'm afraid. She went out.

JILL Oh, I tried to reach her on her mobile phone, but there was no reply.

VERA She didn't take it with her, I'm afraid. She probably forgot. It's here on the desk.

JILL Did she say where she was going?

VERA She didn't say anything, but she should be back soon. She left more than two hours ago. Would you like to leave a message? Or shall I tell her to ring you back?

JILL Could you tell her to ring me back, please? That would be nice. Thank you, Mrs Jones. Bye.

VERA Goodbye, Jill.

Answer the questions.

*1* Where did Emily go?
*2* Why was there no reply on the mobile phone?
*3* When did she leave the house?
*4* What will Vera tell Emily when she comes back?

## 2 Ordering by phone

Alice Richards and Tom Jefferson work for a company which sells bedlinen and other household linens. One day Vera Jones phones the company to place an order.

ALICE Blackwell & Martins Ltd. Good afternoon.

VERA Good afternoon. I'd like to order some items from your summer sales catalogue, please.

ALICE One moment. I'll put you through to our mail-order department. ... I'm sorry, the extension's engaged at the moment. Would you like to wait?

VERA Yes, I'll wait.

...

TOM Blackwell & Martins, mail-order department.

VERA Hello. My name is Vera Jones. I'd like to order some bedlinen from your sales catalogue, please.

TOM Yes, madam. Which articles would you like?

VERA 'Flower Day' duvet covers and pillowcases.

TOM OK. Could you tell me the catalogue number, please?

VERA Um ... that's number J17597, two duvet covers, size 135 × 220cm, item price £34, and number S17597, two pillowcases, standard size, 48 × 73cm, item price £7.

TOM May I repeat: two duvet covers number J17597, size 135 × 220cm, item price £34, and two pillowcases number S17597, standard size, 48 × 73cm, item price £7. Right?

VERA Yes, that's right.

TOM Have you got a customer number?

VERA No, I haven't.

TOM Could you tell me your name and address, then, please?

VERA Vera Jones, 58 Manchuria Road, London SW11.

TOM Sorry, I didn't get the name of the road. Could you spell it, please?

VERA M-A-N-C-H-U-R-I-A.

TOM Yes, thank you, I've got that.

VERA When will the goods arrive?

TOM We'll send them straight away, so you'll have them within two days or so.

VERA All right, that sounds good. Thank you. Goodbye.

TOM Goodbye.

Answer the questions.

1 What does Vera Jones order? Describe the articles.
2 How many items does she order?
3 How much will she have to pay?
4 When will she have the items?

## 3 Working with words

Read or listen to the telephone dialogue again and find the English translation of the following words.

1 Sommerschlussverkauf
2 Katalog
3 verbinden
4 Postversand
5 Abteilung
6 Apparat
7 besetzt
8 bestellen
9 Einzelpreis
10 Größe
11 wiederholen
12 buchstabieren

**ALPHABET AND INTERNATIONAL SPELLING CODE**

| | | | | | |
|---|---|---|---|---|---|
| A | ay | Alpha | N | enn | November |
| B | bee | Bravo | O | oh | Oscar |
| C | see | Charlie | P | pee | Papa |
| D | dee | Delta | Q | queue | Quebec |
| E | ee | Echo | R | are | Romeo |
| F | eff | Foxtrot | S | ess | Sierra |
| G | gee | Golf | T | tee | Tango |
| H | aytch | Hotel | U | you | Uniform |
| I | eye | India | V | vee | Victor |
| J | jay | Juliette | W | double-you | Whisky |
| K | kay | Kilo | X | ex | X-ray |
| L | ell | Lima | Y | why | Yankee |
| M | emm | Mike | Z | zed (AE: zee) | Zulu |

## 4 Spelling

Work with a partner. Spell the following while your partner takes notes:

1 your first name
2 your surname
3 your address
4 a friend's address

## 5 Red velvet hearts

Listen to the dialogue. What are Alice Richards and Fiona Williams talking about? Find the right words.

*a* *heart / hard* shaped
*b* *cushions / cashiers*
*c* *quiet / quite* sure
*d* *fun / front* page of the catalogue
*e* *bright / right* red
*f* a few *left / leave*
*g* the new *live / delivery*

Then listen to the dialogue again and answer these questions.

*1* What did Fiona's friend buy?
*2* Why does Fiona ring the shop?
*3* When did Fiona's friend buy the cushions?
*4* What material are the cushions made of?
*5* Why does Alice ask Fiona to hold on a moment?
*6* Why are they not available at the moment?
*7* When will they get a new delivery?

## 6 Calling back

Write the simple past tense of the words in brackets. Then listen to the dialogue to check your answers.

JILL Hello.

EMILY Hello, Jill. It's Emily. My mother ...1 (tell) me you ...2 (ring) earlier today.

JILL Yes, I ...3 (call) several times. Where ...4 (be) you?

EMILY I ...5 (be) out in Main Street. I ...6 (have) to do some shopping.

JILL What ...7 (you buy)?

EMILY Just a pair of sports shoes, but it ...8 (take) some time to find the right pair.

JILL I actually ...9 (want) to ask you if you'd like to go to the cinema tonight?

EMILY Oh, yes, why not. What would you like to see?

JILL I'm not sure. But I ...10 (think) maybe we could meet at the King's Head at about seven and then we could decide where to go.

EMILY Yes, that's fine with me. See you at the pub then.

## SIMPLE PAST

1 I **wanted** to buy some cushions, too.
2 She probably **forgot**.
3 They **were** on the front page of your catalogue.
4 When **did** she **leave** home?
5 I **didn't get** the name of the road.

- *Bei regelmäßigen Verben bildet man das* simple past, *indem man* -(e)d *an den Infinitiv anfügt (1). Es gibt aber einige Ausnahmen, wie z. B.*
  plan – planned  travel – travelled
  stop – stopped  supply – supplied
- *Unregelmäßige Verben haben für die Vergangenheit eine eigene Form (2, 3).* *Siehe Liste auf Seite 120.*
- *Fragen und Verneinungen im* simple past *werden meist mit* did *gebildet (5, 6). Eine Ausnahme bildet das Verb* be *(siehe unten).*

| **Statements** | **Questions** | **Negatives** |
|---|---|---|
| **Regular verbs** | | |
| I worked | did I work? | I didn't (= did not) work |
| you worked | did you work? | you didn't work |
| he/she/it worked | did he/she/it work? | he/she/it didn't work |
| we worked | did we work? | we didn't work |
| you worked | did you work? | you didn't work |
| they worked | did they work? | they didn't work |
| **Irregular verbs** | | |
| I went | did I go? | I didn't (= did not) go |
| you went | did you go? | you didn't go |
| he/she/it went | did he/she/it go? | he/she/it didn't go |
| we went | did we go? | we didn't go |
| you went | did you go? | you didn't go |
| they went | did they go? | they didn't go |
| **be** | | |
| I was | was I? | I wasn't (= was not) |
| you were | were you? | you weren't (= were not) |
| he/she/it was | was he/she/it? | he/she/it wasn't |
| we were | were we? | we weren't |
| you were | were you? | you weren't |
| they were | were they? | they weren't |

⚠ Achten Sie auf die Aussprache der Endungen:
[d] order**ed**, arriv**ed**  [t] book**ed**, talk**ed**  [ɪd] start**ed**

## 7 Harry's diary

Look at Harry's diary and write some sentences about what he did that week.

## 8 Practice

Match the sentences on the left to the responses on the right.

1 Good morning, ... speaking. Can I speak to ... please?
2 I'm afraid the number is engaged. Is it urgent?
3 Sorry to keep you waiting, but there's no reply.
4 Can I ring her direct?
5 Would you like to leave a message?
6 Thank you very much.

You're welcome. I'll tell him you called.

Hold the line, please, I'll put you through.

No, it isn't. I'll try again later.

Yes, please. Would you mind asking him to ring me? It's urgent.

Oh dear, I've got to get in touch with her today.

Of course. Just dial extension 126.

## 9 Role play

Work with a partner to do some telephone role plays. One of you works for the mail-order department at Blackwell & Martins: use the excerpt from the catalogue in File 6 on page 94 to take the customer's order. The other student plays the role of the customer and makes a phone call. For customer profiles, turn to File 1 on page 92 and File 4 on page 93.

UNIT

# 9 *Souvenirs from abroad*

## 1 Fragile animals

Silvia Möller works in a souvenir shop. A lot of foreign customers come to the shop every day, so she speaks a lot of English.

SILVIA Can I help you?

CUSTOMER These glass animals here are so pretty. How much are they?

SILVIA That depends on the size, sir. This elephant here, for example, is €38.50, these owls are €29 each and that cat over there is €32.70.

CUSTOMER Oh, that's not exactly cheap. Why are they so expensive? They're just glass, aren't they?

SILVIA Not just ordinary glass, sir. They're lead crystal, a very high quality.

CUSTOMER Really? But still …

SILVIA It's a very famous brand, one of our best selling products.

CUSTOMER Well, I'm not sure. May I look around a bit?

SILVIA Of course, sir. Just ask if you need any assistance.

Answer the questions.

*1* Why are the glass animals all different prices?
*2* What material are they made of?
*3* Why are they special?

## 2 A cuckoo clock

SILVIA Can I help you, madam?

CUSTOMER I like this clock here. What is it?

SILVIA It's a cuckoo clock. When the hands on the clock-face show the full hour, the little door opens and the cuckoo comes out. I'll show you. One moment … *(cuckoo–cuckoo–cuckoo)*

CUSTOMER Oh, that's very nice. How does it work? Is there a battery inside?

SILVIA No, it isn't battery operated. It's mechanical. You just have to pull on these chains once a day to keep the clock running. It's quite clever, really.

CUSTOMER I see. Yes, this is very pretty. I'll take this one. Can you pack it for me? I'm going back home tomorrow and I'm afraid it might get damaged on the aeroplane.

SILVIA I'll wrap it up in bubble wrap and put it in a cardboard box. Will that be OK?

CUSTOMER Yes, that will be fine.

SILVIA But perhaps you should take it on the plane as hand luggage, just to make sure.

CUSTOMER Yes, that's a good idea. I'll do that. Uhm … can I pay by credit card?

SILVIA Yes, of course. One moment. Would you sign here, please?

CUSTOMER May I borrow your pen? Thank you.

SILVIA So, here you are, madam. Your receipt and your bag. Thank you. Goodbye. And have a nice trip home.

CUSTOMER Thank you. Goodbye.

> ⚠ lend *heißt (her)borgen, leihen*
> Could you **lend** me your pen?
> borrow *heißt (sich) (aus)borgen, (aus)leihen*
> May I **borrow** your pen?

Are the statements true or false? Correct the false statements.

1 The customer wants to buy a watch.
2 The cuckoo clock is battery operated.
3 Silvia wraps the clock up in paper and puts it in a box.
4 The customer pays cash for the clock.
5 Silvia gives the customer a receipt.

## 3 Working with words

Look at the dialogue in exercise 2 and find the English translations for the following German words.

*1* funktionieren
*2* mechanisch
*3* Kette
*4* beschädigt
*5* einpacken
*6* Luftpolster-Folie
*7* Pappkarton-Schachtel
*8* Handgepäck
*9* sicherzugehen
*10* unterschreiben
*11* (sich) ausborgen/ausleihen
*12* schöne Heimreise!

## 4 More souvenirs to take home

TOM What do you think of this illustrated calendar here, Sue? Do you think my mom would like it?

SUE Let me see. Yes, great pictures. She loves mountains, doesn't she? I'm sure she'll like it. Look at that T-shirt! Isn't that cute?

SILVIA Can I help you?

SUE Yes, we're looking for some gifts for our family at home. What size is that T-shirt?

SILVIA It's medium. But we've got them in small and large as well.

SUE No, medium is fine. We'll take this one, and this calendar here.

SILVIA Anything else?

TOM I'd like to have a look at those sculptures over there. Who are they?

SILVIA They are all famous composers. This one is Wagner, that's Mozart and here are Beethoven and Brahms.

TOM Oh, they're quite heavy. What material is it?

SILVIA It's imitation marble.

TOM What do you think, Sue? Shall we take these two?

SUE Ok, Tom, if you promise to carry them.

SILVIA We could also send them on to you if you like.

TOM No, thank you. They're not that heavy. We'll manage.

| | |
|---|---|
| ⚠ gift | *Geschenk* |
| present | *Geschenk* |
| poison | *Gift* |

Answer the questions.

*1* Who is the calendar for?
*2* What kind of pictures are on the calendar?
*3* What sizes are the T-shirts available in?
*4* Who were Wagner, Mozart, Beethoven and Brahms?
*5* What material are the sculptures made of?
*6* Why does Sue ask Tom to carry them?

## 5 Questions and answers

Match the questions on the left with the answers on the right.

| | |
|---|---|
| 1 I can't find my pen. May I borrow yours? | Yes, this one is very nice. |
| 2 Do you sell stamps? | No, thank you. That's all. |
| 3 Are you paying cash? | Oh, yes, please. I'm afraid it might break. |
| 4 Can I help you? | Yes, please, they are a present for my aunt. |
| 5 Would you like anything else? | Yes, we do, sign here, please. |
| 6 What about these ones? | No, thank you. I'm just looking. |
| 7 Shall I wrap it up? | No, I'd like to pay by credit card. |
| 8 Shall I gift-wrap them? | No, they're not what I am looking for. |
| 9 How do you like this one? | I'm sorry, we don't. But there is a post office across the road. |
| 10 Do you accept credit cards? | Of course, here you are. |

**MORE USEFUL PHRASES**

| Shop assistant | Customer |
|---|---|
| Can I help you? | I'm looking for a ... |
| What can I do for you? | I'd like some ... |
| What about this one? | Have you got any ... |
| How do you like these? | No, I don't really like this one. |
| I'll show you what we've got. | No, I don't like that at all. |
| One moment, I'll show you something else. | These ones are too expensive, I'm afraid. |
| I'll go and get another one. | No, I'm afraid that's not what I'm looking for. |
| Would you like anything else? | Have you got any other ones? |
| May I show you anything else? | Could you show me the red one again? |
| Is there anything else I can do for you? | I prefer the blue one. |
| Would you like a carrier bag? | No, thank you, that's all. |
| How would you like to pay? | I'd like to pay by credit card. |
| I'm afraid we don't accept credit cards. | I'm paying cash. |
| I'm afraid we only accept Visa/Diner's card/... . | Where do I have to sign? |
| Sign here please. | May I borrow your biro please? |
| May I lend you a pen? | Thanks for your advice. |
| Have a nice day. | Thank you for your help/assistance. |

## 6 Dialogue

Look again at the dialogue in exercise 1. In pairs, play the roles of Silvia and the customer and continue the sales dialogue.

GRAMMAR CHECK

## MODAL VERBS

- *Mit modalen Hilfsverben werden Sprechabsichten wie Fähigkeit und Verpflichtung ausgedrückt.* Modal verbs *haben für alle Personen dieselbe Form und werden mit dem Infinitiv ohne* to *verwendet. Es folgen einige Beispiele:*

FÄHIGKEIT
I **can** speak French but I **can't** (= cannot) speak it very well. *(können)*
I **couldn't** speak French when I was 8. *(konnten)*

HÖFLICHE BITTE
**Can** I help you? *(können)*
**Could** you give me a carrier bag? *(könnten)*
**May** I look around a bit? *(dürfen)*

ANGEBOT
**Shall** I wrap it up? *(sollen; Vorsicht: wird nur mit* I *und* we *verwendet)*

RATSCHLAG
You **should** take it on as hand luggage. *(sollen)*

VERPFLICHTUNG/NOTWENDIGKEIT
I **must** go now, it's late. *(müssen)*

FEHLEN EINER NOTWENDIGKEIT
You **needn't** buy any bread, we've got enough. *(nicht müssen/nicht brauchen: Vorsicht: nur als Verneinung)*

VERBOT
You **mustn't** (= must not) smoke in here. *(nicht dürfen)*

MÖGLICHKEIT/ANNAHME
I'm not sure where she is. She **may** be at work. *(könnten)*
She **should** be back soon. *(müßten)*

## 7 Practice

Complete the sentences with the words below. There may be more than one possible answer. Then translate the sentences.

can ◆ cannot
could ◆ shall
should ◆ may
must ◆ need

*1* What are you looking for? ... I help you?
*2* I ... find my purse. It ... be here somewhere.
*3* Here it is. You ... be more careful.
*4* ... I come with you?
*5* You ... not go there now, you ... do that tomorrow.
*6* He ... not speak like that, it is not polite.
*7* There's plenty of time, you ... not hurry.
*8* ... you answer the phone please?
*9* ... I open the window? It's very hot in here.
*10* She ... speak three foreign languages.

| WOULD LIKE/LIKE/WANT/WILL | |
|---|---|
| **would like** *(möchten)*<br>*wird für eine höfliche Frage oder ein Angebot oder für eine Willensäußerung in höflicher Form verwendet.*<br>Would *kann auch mit* love, recommend, suggest *und* prefer *verwendet werden.* | I'**d** (= I **would**) **like** a cup of tea.<br>**Would** you **like** another one?<br>He'**d love** to see that.<br>**I'd prefer** the other one. |
| **like** *(mögen, gefallen)* | How do you **like** this one?<br>She doesn't **like** fish. |
| **want** *(wollen)*<br>*wird für eine Willensäußerung verwendet* | She **wants** to go home now.<br>I don't **want** to do that. |
| **will** *(werden = Zukunft)* | **I'll** (I **will**) go home now.<br>**Will** he help me?<br>I **won't** (**will not**) be home all day. |

## 8 Translation

Translate the sentences into German. Then close the book and translate them back into English. Compare them with the original sentences.

1. We mustn't forget to buy a gift for Sarah.
2. Do you like this sculpture?
3. Do you think Sarah would like it?
4. I'll buy one for her.
5. Do you want to buy it now?
6. We must buy it now.
7. We won't have time tomorrow.
8. She likes Beethoven very much.
9. I'd like this Beethoven sculpture, please.
10. I hope Sarah will like it.

## 9 Welcome to EUROland

The euro is the common currency in many European countries. Do you know which ones? Choose from the countries in the box.

Austria ◆ Belgium
the Czech Republic
Denmark ◆ Finland
France ◆ Germany
Greece ◆ Hungary
Ireland ◆ Italy
Luxembourg
the Netherlands
Poland ◆ Portugal
Slovakia ◆ Spain
Sweden ◆ Switzerland
the UK

*1* Can you find all of the countries above on the map?
*2* What are their capitals?
*3* What languages are spoken there?

## 10 Puzzle

Find the adjectives in the puzzle that go with these countries. Copy them down on a separate piece of paper.

Australia ◆ Canada ◆ China
Croatia ◆ Egypt ◆ Great Britain
Israel ◆ Japan ◆ Mexico
Russia ◆ Switzerland
Turkey ◆ USA

| | | | | | | | | | |
|---|---|---|---|---|---|---|---|---|---|
| N | X | C | H | I | N | E | S | E | S |
| A | C | R | O | A | T | I | A | N | N |
| I | H | N | A | I | S | S | U | R | L |
| D | S | S | I | W | S | B | J | Q | I |
| A | I | I | I | L | E | A | R | S | I |
| N | T | W | W | I | P | Z | J | R | N |
| A | I | D | T | A | F | G | B | P | Z |
| C | R | I | N | A | C | I | X | E | M |
| E | B | E | H | S | I | K | R | U | T |
| H | S | A | M | E | R | I | C | A | N |
| E | N | A | I | T | P | Y | G | E | B |
| A | U | S | T | R | A | L | I | A | N |

UNIT

# 10 At a department store

## 1 Where is it?

Look at the picture and say where you think these departments are.

START LIKE THIS Shoes, bags and leather goods are **on the third floor**.
The household goods and china department is **in the basement**.
The ... department is **on the ground floor**.

books and stationery ◆ carpets
children's wear ◆ cosmetics
electrical goods ◆ fabrics ◆ food
furniture ◆ haberdashery
home textiles
household goods and china
jewellery ◆ ladies' wear ◆ lamps
men's wear ◆ music
restaurant
shoes, bags and leather goods
sports and camping accessories
toilet ◆ toys and games

## 2 Special offers

Draw this chart on a separate piece of paper. Then listen to the CD and write down the seven special offers you hear.

| | article(s) | special offer | department / floor |
|---|---|---|---|
| 1 | | | |
| 2 | | | |
| 3 | | | |
| 4 | | | |
| 5 | | | |

## SHOWING THE WAY

| | | | |
|---|---|---|---|
| go | to the basement<br>to the second floor<br>to the toy department<br>upstairs to the sports department<br>downstairs to the ground floor | you'll find it<br><br><br>it's | in the basement<br>on the first floor<br>in the toy department<br>upstairs on the first floor<br>downstairs in the basement |

## 3 Showing the way

Carol White is at the information desk on the ground floor. Match the information she gives to the customers with their questions. Then listen to the CD to check your answers.

1 Excuse me, where is the toilet?
2 I'd like to buy some buttons and zips. Do you sell these things?
3 Excuse me, where can I buy a doll's house?
4 I'm looking for a pressure cooker. Where can I find one?
5 Excuse me, do you sell mattresses?
6 Can you tell me where I can buy a wrist-watch, please?
7 Excuse me, I'd like to buy a fountain pen. Have you got any?
8 Do you sell oriental rugs?
9 Excuse me, where can I find a tent?

Yes we do. You'll find all kinds of carpets on the fourth floor, next to the furniture. The lift is over there.

In the jewellery department, straight on behind the music department.

You've got to go to the camping department. It's on the third floor.

There's one near the restaurant, on the third floor. You can take the lift over there.

Yes, that's here on the ground floor, in the stationery department.

Yes we do. You'll find them in the furniture department on the top floor. You can take the lift over there.

In the household department, downstairs in the basement. The escalator is out of order, I'm afraid. But you can use the stairs here on the left.

You have to go up to the toy department on the second floor. You can use the lift over there or the escalator here on the right.

Yes, we do. The haberdashery department is on the first floor. There's an escalator here on the right.

## 4 Role play

In pairs, play the roles of Carol White and customers who'd like to do the following things:

buy a CD
try on a pair of jeans
buy a teddy bear
make a phone call
buy a blue silk tie
look at tennis rackets
buy a bottle of suntan lotion
eat a sandwich
buy three bath-towels
buy new batteries for a walkman
buy a bag of onions
look at some girls' jackets
buy a nightdress
look at some gold earrings

## 5 A gift for Anna

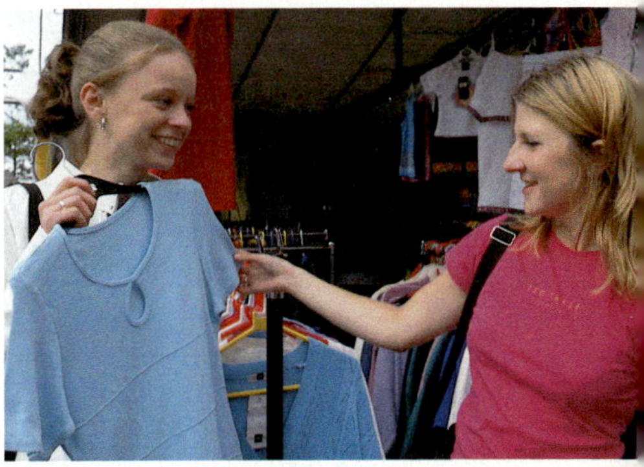

Emily is helping Monika find gifts to take back to her family in Vienna.

MONIKA I like this blue T-shirt better than the black one. What do you think, Emily?

EMILY Yes, it's much prettier. But it's also more expensive, isn't it?

MONIKA No, look it's on special offer. It's even cheaper than the black one. And it's not as big as the other one. I think I'll buy it for my younger sister.

EMILY That's Julia, right? How old is she?

MONIKA No, Julia is two years older than me, the younger one is called Anna. She's 13.

EMILY Oh, yes, that's right. You told me. I got them mixed up. What do your sisters look like?

MONIKA Julia is about as tall as me, but her hair is darker than mine. Anna is nearly as tall as I am and if she keeps on growing like that she'll soon be the tallest of the three of us.

EMILY Has Anna got blond hair as well?

MONIKA No, her hair is darker, like Julia's, but not as straight. She has got curly hair. I'll send you a photograph when I get home.

Are the statements true or false? Correct the false statements.

1 The black T-shirt does not look as nice as the blue one.
2 The blue T-shirt is more expensive than the black one.
3 Monika is younger than Julia.
4 Julia's hair is as dark as Monika's.
5 Anna is taller than her sisters.
6 Anna is the youngest.
7 Julia's hair is not as straight as Anna's.

GRAMMAR CHECK

### COMPARISON OF ADJECTIVES AND ADVERBS

*1* It's even **cheaper** than the black one.
*2* She'll soon be the **tallest** of the three of us.
*3* She is much **prettier** than I am.
*4* I prefer a **more modern** style.
*5* But it's also **more expensive**, isn't it?
*6* This T-shirt costs **less** than the other one.
*7* It's not **as big as** the other one.

- *Einsilbige Adjektive (1, 2) und zweisilbige Adjektive, die auf* -y *enden (3), werden mit* -(i)er / -(i)est *gesteigert.*
- *Die meisten zweisilbigen Adjektive (4), alle mehrsilbigen Adjektive (5) und Adverbien mit der Endung* -ly *werden mit* more/most *gesteigert.*
- *Einige Adjektive bzw. Adverbien haben unregelmäßige Steigerungsformen, z. B.:*

| | | |
|---|---|---|
| good/well | better | best |
| bad/badly | worse | worst |
| little (= *wenig*) | less | least |
| much/many | more | most |

⚠ *Wenn Sie Personen oder Sachen im Satz vergleichen, benutzen Sie nach einem Komparativ das Wort* than *(1, 3, 6).*
*Beachten Sie:* (not) as ... as = *(nicht) so ... wie (7).*

## 6 Which car is best?

Use the following words to compare the cars.

old ◆ new ◆ cheap ◆ expensive ◆ big ◆ small ◆ beautiful
good ◆ bad ◆ fast ◆ comfortable

**SALE**

**1997 model**

**€3500**

**SALE**

**1988 model**

**€6000**

**SALE**

**New model**

**€12000**

## 7 Where the money goes

Look at the table showing how much money people in different countries spend on food, housing, etc and write seven sentences about it. Use more/less/the most/the least.

EXAMPLES People in Austria spend more on food but less on health than people in Germany. People in Greece spend the most on food, but the least on fuel and power.

**Household spending in percentages (some European countries)**

| | Germany | Britain | Austria | Sweden | Greece |
|---|---|---|---|---|---|
| Food | 11 | 11 | 15 | 15 | 30 |
| Alcohol and tobacco | 4 | 9 | 4 | 5 | 7 |
| Clothes | 7 | 6 | 8 | 6 | 8 |
| Things for the home (furniture etc) | 8 | 7 | 8 | 7 | 7 |
| Transport and communication | 15 | 17 | 16 | 16 | 15 |
| Housing (eg rent) | 17 | 16 | 15 | 28 | 11 |
| Fuel and power (gas, electricity etc) | 3 | 4 | 4 | 5 | 2 |
| Leisure | 9 | 10 | 8 | 9 | 5 |
| Health (eg medical insurance) | 16 | 2 | 7 | 2 | 4 |
| Other | 10 | 18 | 15 | 7 | 11 |

## 8 The most famous department store?

Complete the text with the words below.

after ◆ biggest ◆ famous ◆ later ◆ located ◆ more ◆ popular
small ◆ visit ◆ work

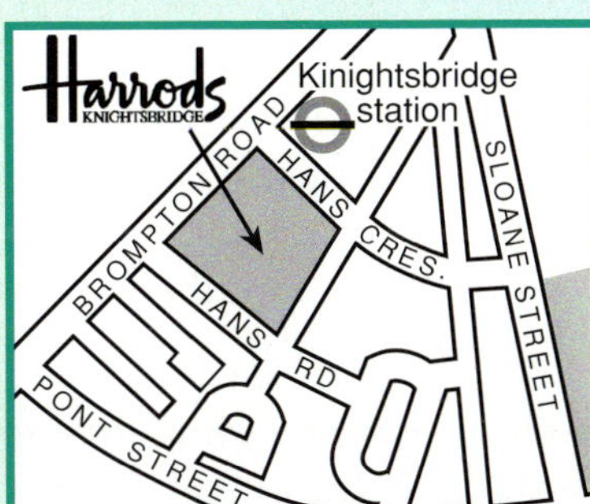


To get to Harrods by underground take the Piccadilly Line to Knightsbridge.

*Or go by bus:*
Brompton Road, 14, 74, C1, A1 (airbus)
Sloane Street, 19, 22, 137

*Harrods is open from*
10 a.m. to 6 p.m. Monday, Tuesday and Saturday
10 a.m. to 7 p.m. Wednesday, Thursday and Friday
*There are special Christmas opening hours.*

**Harrods**, ...1 in Knightsbridge in West London, started out as a ...2 grocer and tea merchant in East London back in 1834. One hundred and fifty years ...3, Harrods is the ...4 department store in Europe and the world's most ...5 shop. Four thousand people ...6 there and ...7 than 50,000 people ...8 the store every day. It is the third most ...9 tourist attraction in London ...10 St. Paul's and Big Ben.

## 9 Giving directions

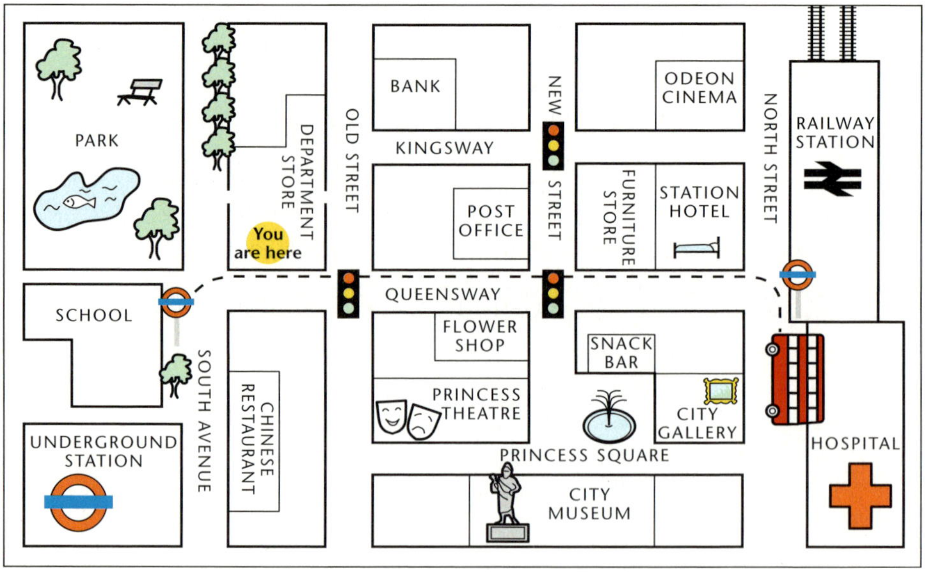


Sometimes Carol White also gives directions to places outside the department store. Read or listen to the dialogues and follow the routes on your map.

CUSTOMER Excuse me, do you sell stamps?

CAROL No, I'm sorry, we don't. But there's a post office in New Street.

CUSTOMER Could you tell me the way, please?

CAROL Certainly, take the exit to Old Street and cross the road. Turn left and take the first street on the right. Turn right again at the next corner, and the post office is there.

CUSTOMER Is it very far?

CAROL No, it's only about five minutes' walk.

...

CUSTOMER Excuse me, how do I get to the railway station from here?

CAROL Do you want to walk? You can also take the bus if you like.

CUSTOMER I prefer the bus. I've got quite a lot of things to carry.

CAROL Well, the bus stop is in South Avenue. Cross the road when you leave the shop. Turn left and walk until you see the school. There's a bus stop in front of it. The number 58 goes directly to the railway station.

Now work with a partner and take turns asking for and giving directions to the following places. Start at the underground station.

| | |
|---|---|
| to the City Gallery | a bank |
| the department store | the theatre |
| the nearest hotel | the hospital |

**ASKING FOR AND GIVING DIRECTIONS**

Excuse me, how do I get to the hospital from here?
Do you know a restaurant near here?

Yes, there is one in East Street.
It's not far, you can walk.
It's quite far, you'd better take the bus / the underground / a taxi.
Get on the (number) 58, in the direction of Paddington Station.
Change at the hospital to the (number) 72.
Get off at the third bus stop.
Go to the end of the street.
Go as far as the traffic lights.
Turn right at the junction of North Street and South Street.
Take the third street on your left.
Walk along East Street as far as the post office.
Cross West Street.
It's just across the street.

## 10 Role play

A tourist has got one day to visit your town. Think of some interesting places to visit and find the best route to see them using public transport.

## 11 Puzzle

Read the clues and find out what is where in Main Street.

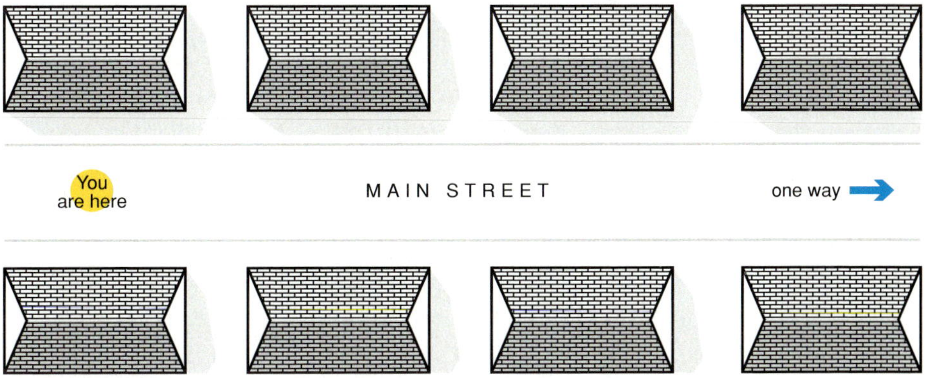


The museum is the last building on the left.
The restaurant is the second building on the right.
The post office is between the cinema and the restaurant.
The bank is opposite the railway station.
The school is not next to the museum.
The school is next to the railway station.
And where is the flower shop?

UNIT

# 11 *Fashion matters*

## 1 In the ladies' wear department

SHOP ASSISTANT Can I help you?

CUSTOMER I'm looking for a blouse, but these are too big, I'm afraid.

SHOP ASSISTANT What's your size, madam?

CUSTOMER Size 12, I think.

SHOP ASSISTANT These ones here are size 16, size 12 is on the rack over there. What style and colour are you looking for?

CUSTOMER Something to match my jeans. Some light pastel colour perhaps.

SHOP ASSISTANT Do you prefer long sleeves or short sleeves?

CUSTOMER I'd rather have a long-sleeved one.

SHOP ASSISTANT What about this pale blue pinstriped one? Or here's a nice patterned one, and here's a plain white one. They would all look great with blue jeans.

CUSTOMER Hmm, I like the white one. What material is it?

SHOP ASSISTANT One moment, I'll have a look. It's made of pure linen.

CUSTOMER But that's so difficult to iron, isn't it?

SHOP ASSISTANT The label says here it should be ironed at a very high temperature. It's best to iron it while it's still damp. Then it's quite easy.

CUSTOMER Well, I'm not sure. What material are the others?

SHOP ASSISTANT The blue striped one is a cotton-synthetic mixture. You can wash it at 60° and it's easy to iron. The yellow patterned one is 100 per cent cotton. And here is another white one. It's silk, but it can also be washed in the washing machine.

| | |
|---|---|
| CUSTOMER | Yes, it looks nice. Can I try this white one and the one with the pinstripes? |
| SHOP ASSISTANT | Certainly, madam. The fitting room is over there. |
| SHOP ASSISTANT | How were they? |
| CUSTOMER | The sizes are all right, but I don't think the white one really suits me, it makes me look so pale. I think I'll take this one. |

Answer the questions.

1 What kind of blouse is the customer looking for?
2 What size does she need?
3 What pattern does the pale blue blouse have?
4 What does the pure cotton one look like?
5 What colour is the linen blouse?
6 How should the linen blouse be ironed?
7 How can the silk blouse be washed?
8 Do the blouses fit the customer?
9 Do the blouses suit her?
10 Which one does she buy?

## 2 Colours and patterns

Match the words with the pictures.

red ◆ pink ◆ orange ◆ brown ◆ yellow ◆ cream ◆ blue
turquoise ◆ navy ◆ purple ◆ light green ◆ dark green
black ◆ white ◆ grey ◆ striped ◆ polka-dot ◆ check
tartan ◆ patterned

## 3 Care instructions

Match the care instructions to the symbols.

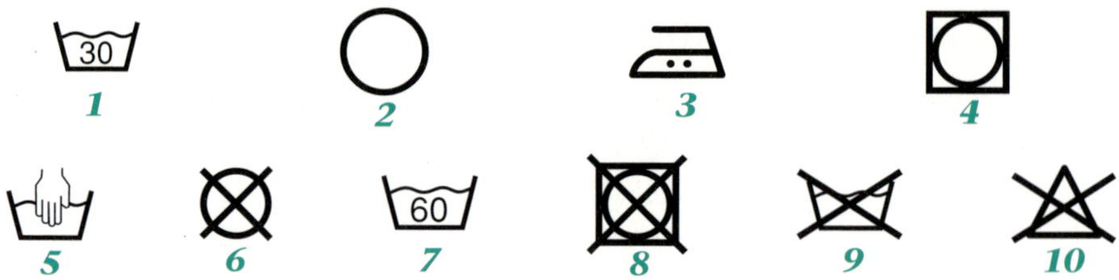


You can wash it in the washing machine at 60°C.
It says here you can tumble-dry it.
You should not put in the tumble-dryer.
It's pure wool, so it should be hand-washed.
It should be ironed on a medium setting.
It should be dry-cleaned.
The label says it must not be dry-cleaned.
It must not be washed.
It can be washed at 30°C.
It must not be bleached.

**GRAMMAR CHECK**

### PASSIVE WITH MODALS

*1* It **can be washed** in the washing machine.
*2* It **must be ironed** at a high temperature.

- *Passivsätze mit modalen Hilfsverben werden mit einem modalen Hilfsverb +* be *+ Partizip Perfekt (3. Form) gebildet. Für die Verwendung der Zeitformen gelten die gleichen Regeln wie im Aktiv.*
- *Durch den Gebrauch des Passivs wird das Prädikat hervorgehoben. Das Passiv wird oft verwendet, wenn die beschriebene Handlung wichtiger ist als die Person/Sache, die diese Handlung ausführt.*

## 4 Practice

Rewrite the sentences in the passive form.

*1* You must not wash this jacket.
*2* You should dry-clean it.
*3* You can wash the jeans at 60° in the washing machine.
*4* You can put them in the tumble-dryer.
*5* You can iron them on a high setting.
*6* You should wash the jumper by hand.
*7* You should not put it into the tumble-dryer.

## 5 In the men's wear department

| | |
|---|---|
| CUSTOMER | Hello. I'm looking for a pair of jeans. May I look around? |
| SHOP ASSISTANT | Certainly. Do you know your size? |
| CUSTOMER | 32, I think, or maybe 34. |
| SHOP ASSISTANT | OK. And what colour do you prefer? |
| CUSTOMER | I like these stonewashed ones here. |
| SHOP ASSISTANT | All these are size 32 and those are all size 34. OK? Let me know if you need anything. |
| | … |
| SHOP ASSISTANT | Have you found anything you like? |
| CUSTOMER | Yes, I'd like to try on these two pairs please. |
| SHOP ASSISTANT | Certainly. The fitting room is over there. |
| | … |
| SHOP ASSISTANT | How are they? |
| CUSTOMER | These button-fly jeans fit well around the waist, but they are a bit too short. Have you got any longer ones? |
| SHOP ASSISTANT | Just a minute. I'll have a look. |
| | … |
| SHOP ASSISTANT | What about the zip-fly ones. Do they fit? |
| CUSTOMER | Well, the size is OK, but I don't like the style. They're too tight. |
| SHOP ASSISTANT | Well, here's another pair of button-fly jeans. They're one inch longer, so they should fit. |
| CUSTOMER | Thank you. I'll try them on. |

Answer the questions.

*1* What kind of jeans is the customer looking for?

*2* Describe the two pairs he tries on.

### TYPES OF JEANS

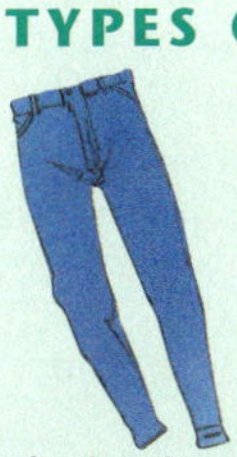
drainpipe

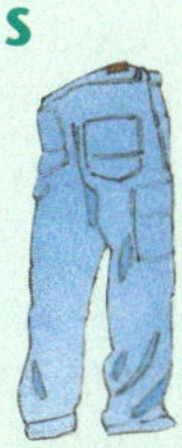
baggy

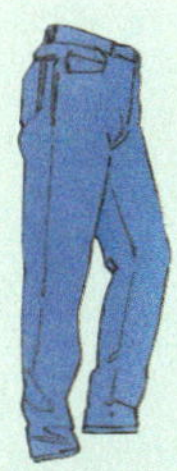
straight

boot leg

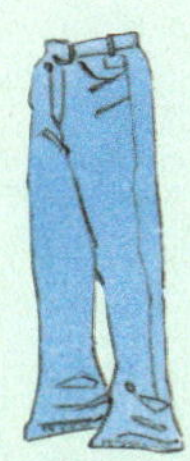
loose cut

⚠ Jeans are sometimes measured in inches. (One inch is about 2.5cm.) You measure the waist and the length.

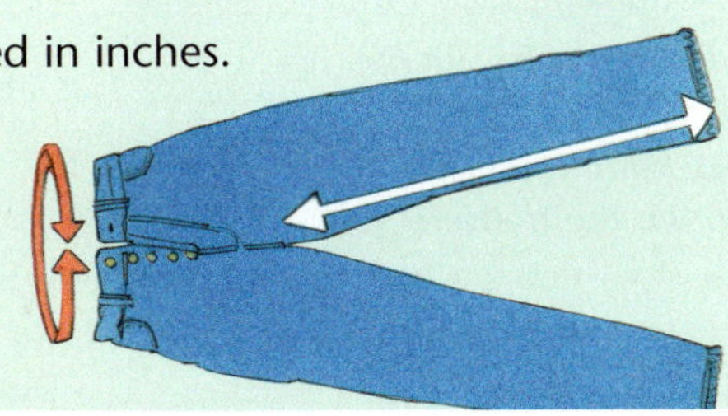

## SIZES

**Women's clothes**

| | | | | | | | | |
|---|---|---|---|---|---|---|---|---|
| European size | 36 | 38 | 40 | 42 | 44 | 46 | 48 | 50 |
| British size | 8 | 10 | 12 | 14 | 16 | 18 | 20 | 22 |
| USA | 6 | 8 | 10 | 12 | 14 | 16 | 18 | 20 |

**Men's shirts**

| | | | | | | | | |
|---|---|---|---|---|---|---|---|---|
| European size | 36 | 37 | 38 | 39 | 40 | 41 | 42 | 43 |
| British size | 14 | 14 | 15 | 15 | 16 | 16 | 17 | 17 |

**Men's suits**

| | | | | |
|---|---|---|---|---|
| European size | 94–97 | 99–102 | 104–107 | 109–112 |
| British size | 37–38 | 39–40 | 41–42 | 43–44 |
| USA | 38 | 40 | 42 | 44 |

**Shoes**

| | | | | | | | |
|---|---|---|---|---|---|---|---|
| European size | 36–37 | 38 | 39–40 | 40–41 | 42 | 43 | 44 |
| British size | 4 | 5 | 6 | 7 | 8 | 9 | 10 |
| USA | 5 | 6 | 7 | 8 | 9 | 10 | 11 |

## 6 Trying on clothes

Match the sentences on the left to the responses on the right.

1 Do the trousers fit you?
2 What about this pink one here?
3 Is the dress the right size?
4 What colour and style are you looking for?
5 Would you like a matching tie?
6 The trousers are a bit too long, I'm afraid. What do you think?
7 This dress is a bit too small I'm afraid. May I try another one?
8 Can I try them on?
9 Where can I try it on please?
10 How does the jacket fit, sir?
11 It doesn't really suit me, it's too dark.
12 How long does it take to shorten the trousers?

One moment, I'll bring you one in a lighter colour.

That's no problem, we can make them shorter for you.

The fitting room is here on the left, madam.

No, thank you. I'll just take the shirt.

Two days. You can pick them up the day after tomorrow.

They are a bit too loose around the waist.

It's a bit too tight around the shoulders.

Yes, it fits perfectly.

Something to match my trousers.

Certainly, the fitting room is just here.

One moment, I'll bring you one in a larger size.

No, I'm afraid that colour doesn't suit me.

## FIT MATCH SUIT

**Fit** *heißt ‚passen in Bezug auf die Größe'.*
Does it **fit** you?
It **fits** very well. It's the right size.

**Match** *heißt ‚passen zu'.*
I'm looking for a blouse to **match** my jeans.
Would you like a **matching** jacket?

**Suit** *heißt ‚passen in Bezug auf Stil oder Farbe' = ‚(gut) stehen'.*
Pink doesn't **suit** me. It makes me look so pale.
I think this style **suits** you very well.

⚠ **Suit** *heißt auch ‚Anzug'!*

## 7 All about clothes

Match the words with the pictures.

bag ◆ belt ◆ blouse ◆ boots ◆ briefcase ◆ cardigan ◆ crop top ◆ dress
high heels ◆ jacket ◆ jeans ◆ jumper ◆ leggings ◆ pocket ◆ polo-neck
round neck ◆ sandals ◆ scarf ◆ shirt ◆ shoes ◆ skirt ◆ sleeve ◆ socks ◆ suit
sweatshirt ◆ tie ◆ tights ◆ tracksuit ◆ tracksuit bottoms ◆ trainers
trousers ◆ T-shirt ◆ vest

## 8 A fashion show

Listen to the CD and say which two models the announcer is describing. Then describe what the other two models are wearing to your partner.

**TOO/RATHER**

| | |
|---|---|
| This shirt is **too** small. | *Dieses Hemd ist zu klein.* |
| This shirt is small, **too**. | *Dieses Hemd ist auch klein.* |
| This skirt is **rather** pale. | *Dieser Rock ist ziemlich hell.* |
| I'd **rather** have a darker one. | *Ich hätte lieber einen dunkleren.* |

## 9 Practice

Choose the correct word to complete each sentence.

fit ◆ fits ◆ match ◆ matches ◆ matching ◆ rather ◆ rather
size ◆ suit ◆ suits ◆ too ◆ too

*1* This skirt doesn't … me. It's … small.
*2* This one is one … larger. It … perfectly.
*3* So, I'll take this green blouse and I think I'll take the yellow one, … .
*4* This coat is … long. I'd … have a shorter coat.
*5* I'm looking for a pair of shoes to … my skirt.
*6* I think this scarf … the colour of your coat well.
*7* Would you like a … hat to go with the scarf?
*8* The style of that dress … you very well. You should buy it.
*9* I like this polo-neck, but grey doesn't really … me.

## 10 Translation

Translate the following sentences into German. Then close the book and translate them back into English. Check with the original sentences.

1. These trousers don't fit me. They're too small.
2. I like the colour of these jeans but I don't like the style.
3. The jacket doesn't fit me. Can you bring me one in a smaller size?
4. Would you like to try on a matching jacket?
5. How do you like this green one?
6. I really don't like green, it doesn't suit me.
7. This one is smaller, I think it will fit me.
8. I'd like a striped shirt with long sleeves.
9. I'd like a shirt with a button-down collar.
10. I like wearing jeans and T-shirts but I never wear suits.
11. This skirt here is the right size and it also suits you very well.
12. I like the style of this jumper here, but have you got it in any other colours?
13. This tie matches the colour of your shirt very well.

## 11 Role play

Follow the instructions to do a role play at a clothing shop.

| **Customer** | **Shop assistant** |
| --- | --- |
| **1** Sie möchten einen Pullover kaufen. | |
| | **2** Fragen Sie nach der Größe und nach der Farbe. |
| **3** Sagen Sie, welche Farben Ihnen gefallen und sagen Sie, dass Sie die Größe nicht genau wissen. | |
| | **4** Zeigen Sie Pullover in verschiedenen Farben und Mustern in zwei verschiedenen Größen. |
| **5** Ihnen gefallen mehrere Pullover. Sagen Sie, dass Sie sie probieren möchten. | |
| | **6** Zeigen sie dem Kunden/der Kundin, wo der Probierraum ist. Fragen Sie, ob etwas passt. |
| **7** Sagen Sie, dass der Rollkragenpullover Ihnen von der Größe und vom Schnitt gut passt, aber dass Ihnen die Farbe leider nicht steht. Fragen Sie, ob es diesen Pullover auch in anderen Farben gibt. | |
| | **8** Sagen Sie, dass Sie nachsehen werden. |

How does the story go on? Think of an ending.

UNIT

# 12 Solving problems

## 1 At the shoe shop

CUSTOMER Excuse me, I've got a problem. Can you help me?

SHOP ASSISTANT I hope so. What's the problem?

CUSTOMER Well, you see, I bought these boots here in your shop about two months ago. And now both soles have come off. I've only had them since February.

SHOP ASSISTANT Oh dear. Did you buy them in our shop?

CUSTOMER Well, it was another branch, but your company. I've got the receipt here somewhere. One moment. Here you are.

SHOP ASSISTANT I see. That's no problem. We can repair them for you. But I'll have to send them to our repair shop. You can pick them up at the end of next week. Will that be OK?

CUSTOMER That would be fine. Will it cost anything?

SHOP ASSISTANT No, it's free. They're still under guarantee. Could you just give me your name and phone number, please?

CUSTOMER Yes, that's Nancy Norman …

Answer the questions

1 When did Nancy buy the boots?
2 What is wrong with them?
3 Where did she buy them?
4 Where will they be repaired?
5 When can she pick them up?
6 How much will it cost?

## 2 At the electronics shop

SHOP ASSISTANT Good morning. May I help you?

CUSTOMER Morning. Yes, please. I've got this CD player here which I bought in your shop some time ago. And now it doesn't work properly.

SHOP ASSISTANT What is wrong with it?

CUSTOMER It just plays the first two or three songs on the CD and then it stops.

SHOP ASSISTANT Does this problem just happen with one CD or have you tried different ones?

CUSTOMER No, it does that with all my CDs and I've had some of them for years. You see, the CD player worked all right when I bought it. But it hasn't worked properly for the last week or so.

SHOP ASSISTANT I can send it back to the manufacturer for you, if you like, and they can have a look at it. When did you say you bought it?

CUSTOMER About two years ago. I'm afraid I've lost the receipt.

SHOP ASSISTANT In this case it doesn't matter. Your guarantee has expired anyway. So, would you like to have it repaired?

CUSTOMER Well, it depends how much it will cost, of course.

SHOP ASSISTANT I could ask for an estimate if you like and then you can decide whether you want it repaired or not. It will take a few days. You can ring us if you like.

CUSTOMER Okay, I'll do that. Can you give me your telephone number, please?

SHOP ASSISTANT It's here on this form. I just need your name and address, please. …

Answer the questions.

1. Why does the customer complain about the CD player?
2. What exactly is wrong with it?
3. Does the problem happen with just one CD?
4. When did the problems start?
5. When did the customer buy the CD player?
6. What has happened to the receipt?
7. What does the shop assistant suggest?
8. When will the shop assistant know how much it will cost?

# Consumer rights

## CONSUMER RIGHTS

Once an article has been bought, shops do not have to take it back as long as the article is all right. But shops usually take back or exchange articles within a few days, if

- ☞ the customer has got the receipt
- ☞ the customer has still got the original packaging
- ☞ the article has not yet been worn or used
- ☞ the article has not been reduced in price

If an article turns out to be faulty, the customer has a right to have it exchanged or repaired. If that is not possible he/she can get a refund. There are different lengths of guarantee depending on the type of goods.

## 3 Dealing with complaints

First read the text on consumer rights above. Then read the beginnings of the dialogues below. How should they continue?

A Excuse me, I bought this video here yesterday, but I'd like to exchange it for another one. Is that possible? I've got the receipt here.

B May I have a look?

A …

A I'd like to exchange these baby trousers. They don't fit my daughter, they are too small. May I have a bigger pair?

B But they look as if she has worn them.

A …

A I bought this T-shirt here two days ago and I'd like to return it. You see, I don't like it after all. Can I have my money back?

B May I see the receipt?

A …

## 4 At the fashion boutique

Put these boxes below into the correct order and read the dialogue.

| Shop assistant | Customer |
| --- | --- |
| **a** Well, I can't give you the money back, I'm afraid, but I can give you the same one in a larger size. | **b** Well, I know. But I only bought it this morning, and she hasn't worn it. She has only tried it on and it doesn't fit her. |
| **c** But this article was on sale. We don't take back articles that are reduced in price, I'm afraid. You see, it even says so on the receipt. | **d** I hope so. You see, I've just bought this blouse as a present for my sister, but unfortunately it doesn't fit her. It's too small. Could I return it? I've got the receipt. |
| **e** Can I help you? | **f** OK, that would be fine. Thank you. |

GRAMMAR CHECK

### SIMPLE PAST OR PRESENT PERFECT

*1* I**'ve** (= I **have**) **had** some of the CDs for years.
*2* I**'ve** just **bought** this T-shirt.
*3* The soles **have come** off.
*4* I **bought** these boots two months ago.

- *Das* present perfect *wird mit* have/has *und dem Partizip Perfekt (3. Form) gebildet (1–3).*
- *Das* present perfect *steht für Vorgänge, die von der Vergangenheit bis in die Gegenwart reichen (1) und wird auch verwendet, wenn eine Handlung soeben* (just) *vollendet wurde (2). Es steht auch, wenn bei einer vergangenen Handlung nicht der Zeitpunkt des Vorgangs, sondern dessen Auswirkung in der Gegenwart betont werden soll (3). Signalwörter für das* present perfect *sind u. a.* just, already, yet, for, since.
- *Im* simple past *wird dagegen ein in der Vergangenheit vollständig abgeschlossener Vorgang geschildert (4). Es wird häufig mit einer Zeitangabe der Vergangenheit (*yesterday, three days ago *usw.) verwendet.*

## 5 Practice

Complete with the present perfect form of the verbs in brackets. Be careful with the word order.

*1* I ... (just buy) this milk here, but it ... (go) off.
*2* It ... (not/expire) yet.
*3* ... (Chris/clean) the shop window yet?
*4* Yes, I think he ... (just/finish).
*5* I'm very hungry. I ... (not/have) my lunch yet.
*6* ... (you/check) the blouses on the special offers rack yet?
*7* No, ... (I/not/have) time for it yet.
*8* Look, what ... (she/do)! She ... (put) all these boots here on the wrong shelf.

## 6 Practice

Complete with the simple past or present perfect form of the verbs in brackets.

*1* The customer ... (leave) half an hour ago.
*2* I ... (not/see) Sharon for at least three years.
*3* She ... (live) in the USA since 1999.
*4* I ... (buy) this TV-set yesterday.
*5* I ... (not have) the time yet to see if it works.
*6* ... (ever/be) to California?
*7* Fiona ... (spend) her holiday in California last year.
*8* ... (already/hear) what ... (happen)?
*9* No, ... (I/not). I ... (just/arrive).
*10* I ... (never/see) anything like that!

**APOLOGIZING**

I'm sorry about this mistake.
I'm very sorry for the long delay.
I'm awfully sorry that this has happened.
I'll give you another one.
May I offer you a discount?
I'll see what I can do.
I cannot give you the money back but I can give you a credit note for the same amount.
I'm not sure what I can do in this case, I'll have to speak to the manager.
One moment, I'll get the manager.
We can't take back articles that have already been worn.
There is nothing we can do about it.

## 7 More complaints

First match the complaints on the left with the shop assistant's replies on the right. Then think of one or two sentences for each case to continue the conversation.

1 I've just bought this loaf of bread. When I opened it at home I saw it was mouldy.

2 This wine tastes peculiar. I think it is off, but I've only just opened it.

3 I've got this fountain pen I bought in your shop but unfortunately it scratches.

4 I washed this tablecloth and look what has happened! It has shrunk even though you said it was shrink resistant.

5 My washing machine does not work properly. It does not spin dry.

6 These are not my photos in this bag!

7 When will my new sofa be delivered? I ordered it three weeks ago, but I haven't received it yet.

At which temperature did you wash it?

Is it possible that you have dropped it?

We'll send you someone to repair it. When will you be at home?

Oh, dear. Maybe the films have been mixed up.

It will be delivered next Tuesday. I'm sorry for the delay.

I'm sorry, maybe the cork was not in properly.

I'm sorry. It must have been packed when it was still hot.

## 8 Practice

Complete the sentences with the most suitable word.

| |
|---|
| ago ◆ by ◆ for ◆ free ◆ just ◆ next ◆ off ◆ off<br>since ◆ still ◆ yet ◆ yet |

*1* It has been three weeks … I ordered it.
*2* I bought these boots two months … .
*3* You will be able to pick them up … the end of next week.
*4* Has the sofa been delivered … ?
*5* It's … under guarantee.
*6* It will be delivered … Tuesday.
*7* It has not worked properly … the last week or two.
*8* It won't cost anything. It will be … .
*9* The soles have come … .
*10* I'm afraid it has not arrived … .
*11* I've … opened the bottle.
*12* It tastes bad. I think it is … .

## 9 Working with words

Complete the sentences with the most suitable word from the box.

| |
|---|
| branch ◆ case ◆ complaints ◆ depends ◆ exchange ◆ expired occur ◆ manufacturer ◆ receipt ◆ reduced ◆ worked |

*1* I'm afraid we can't repair it here. We have to send it to the … .
*2* Your guarantee has … .
*3* We do not take back articles that have been … in price.
*4* I have lost the …, I'm afraid. But I'm sure I bought it here.
*5* I bought it in another … of your company.
*6* Shop assistants sometimes have to deal with … .
*7* It … how much it will cost.
*8* It … all right when I bought it.
*9* Does this problem … with other CDs?
*10* In this … it does not matter.
*11* We can … the article.

GRAMMAR CHECK

### SINCE/FOR/AGO

*1* I've had these shoes **since** May.
*2* I have had them **for** some time.
*3* I bought these boots two months **ago**.

**Since** *(seit) bezeichnet den Zeitpunkt, an dem eine Handlung begonnen hat.*
**For** *(seit) drückt die Dauer der Handlung aus.*
**Ago** *(vor) bezeichnet einen zurückliegenden Zeitraum.*

- *Beachten Sie: Um auszudrücken, dass ein Vorgang in der Gegenwart noch andauert, gebraucht man im Englischen das* present perfect, *im Deutschen dagegen die Gegenwart.*

## 10 Practice

Copy these sentences into your exercise book and complete them with *for / since / ago.*

*1* I have only had it … two weeks.
*2* I bought this CD player two months … .
*3* It worked all right … the first couple of days.
*4* The problem first occurred about two weeks … .
*5* He has been here … two hours.
*6* He has been here … 2 o'clock.
*7* They went to Italy two years … .
*8* I've been waiting … three months.
*9* She has changed a lot … I last saw her.

*10* She has worked ... SNIPS ... 1997.
*11* I started working there a long time ... .
*12* She has lived in Salzburg ... she was born.

## 11 Puzzle

Find the matching verb for each noun. (Write them down on a separate piece of paper.) Then use all the verbs you have found to tell a story.

apology ◆ complaint ◆ decision ◆ delay ◆ delivery ◆ dependence estimate ◆ expiry ◆ reduction ◆ suggestion

| | | | | | | | |
|---|---|---|---|---|---|---|---|
| V | D | E | L | A | Y | N | R |
| Z | N | D | E | P | E | N | D |
| P | I | C | K | O | T | T | D |
| E | A | E | E | L | A | S | E |
| C | L | D | R | O | M | E | L |
| U | P | I | I | G | I | G | I |
| D | M | C | P | I | T | G | V |
| E | O | E | X | Z | S | U | E |
| R | C | D | E | E | E | S | R |

## 12 Role play

Work with a partner to practise making complaints and finding solutions. Student A turn to File 2 on page 92, student B turn to File 7 on page 95. Then think of complaints in your own shop and do some more role plays with a partner.

# Business correspondence

## 1 Form and layout of a business letter

Read the letter on page 89 and answer the questions below.

*1* What are the abbreviations (or symbols) for the following?

- limited company
- for the attention of
- catalogue number
- reference
- per cent

*2* What are the English words for the following?

- Bestellung
- Angebot
- dankbar
- liefern
- Waren, Posten
- vereinbart
- Listenpreis
- Rabatt
- Skonto
- Zahlung
- Lieferung
- sich freuen auf
- mit freundlichen Grüßen

*3* Is Pat Norman a man or a woman? How do you know?

inside address (address of firm the letter is to)

letterhead (address of firm the letter is from)

***the wine cellar ltd***

32 Palace Gardens London SW6 7HJ England
Tel +44 (0) 2073459861 Fax +44 (0) 2073459866

Fratelli Ciccone SPA
attn Mr Guiseppe Fellini
Via San Francesco 21
53100 Siena
Italy

Your ref GF/re
Our ref PN/wk — reference

Date 15 September 20.. — date

Dear Mr Fellini — salutation

subject line — **Order No 1530**

Many thanks for your offer to supply us with Italian wines dated 3 September. We would be grateful if you could supply the following items:

**1** 80 bottles Chianti Classico, Cat. No. D 884 à €7.70
**2** 80 bottles Valpolicella, Cat. No. D 884 à €4.80
**3** 50 bottles Bardolino, Cat. No. D 889 à €5.90
**4** 50 bottles Lambrusco, Cat. No. D 889 à €6.10
**5** 70 bottles Soave, Cat. No. A 501 à €4.95
**6** 70 bottles Frascati, Cat. No. A 581 à €5.20
**7** 40 bottles Orvieto, Cat. No. A 538 à €7.10

As agreed, you are willing to offer us a trade discount of 15% on list price and a further cash discount of 2% if payment is made in full within 15 days of delivery.

Thank you for your assistance. We look forward to receiving the goods shortly.

Yours sincerely — complimentary close
***the wine cellar ltd***

Pat Norman

signature block

Pat Norman (Ms)

## PARTS OF A BUSINESS LETTER

**Letterhead**

A letterhead usually shows the company's name and address, its telephone and fax numbers and its e-mail or Website address.

**Inside address**

The inside address shows the name and address of the firm or person you are writing to. This should be exactly the same as the address you use on the envelope.

| | |
|---|---|
| Mr Frank Millward | Mrs Sarah Stone |
| 34 Grafton Road | 433 Santa Monica Boulevard |
| West Looe | Los Angeles, CA 10067 |
| Cornwall PL13 2BJ | |

In British addresses the postcode comes after the county (in this case Cornwall); in American addresses the ZIP code comes after the state abbreviation.

**Reference**

When you answer a letter from another firm, give the reference of the original letter under **Your Ref:** and your own reference under **Our Ref:** The reference usually gives the initials of the person who wrote the letter and of the person who typed it.

**Date**

You can write dates the following ways

| | |
|---|---|
| GB 3 September 20.. | 3rd September 20.. |
| USA September 3, 20.. | September 3rd, 20.. |

Never use just numbers, for example 3.9.00. In Europe this always means 3 September 2000, but in America and in many Asian countries it can mean 9 March 2000.

**Salutation and complimentary close**

You start a letter with a salutation and finish it with a complimentary close.

| | **salutation** | **complimentary close** |
|---|---|---|
| to a firm | Dear Sir or Madam | Yours faithfully (GB) |
| | Gentlemen (USA) | Yours truly / Truly yours (USA) |
| to a person | Dear Mr Fox | Yours sincerely (GB) |
| | Dear Ms Jones | Sincerely yours (USA) |

Use Miss for an unmarried woman and Mrs for a married woman, or use Ms for either.

**Subject line**

We often use a subject line to say in a few words what the letter is about.

**Signature block**

The firm's name often comes directly above the signature and the sender's name directly after it.

**Special notes**

| | |
|---|---|
| (For the) Attention of Mr Paul Fox | *zu Händen von Herrn Paul Fox* |
| Confidential | *Vertraulich* |
| Private and Confidential | *Persönlich und Vertraulich* |
| Registered | *Eingeschrieben* |
| Urgent | *Dringend* |

## 2 Addresses

Correct the mistakes. There is one mistake in each address.

*1* Ms Williams Fiona
123 Cromwell Road
London SW7 4ET

*2* Mr.
Charles Chapman
109 Main Street
Carson City, NV 89710

*3* Classic Bikes Ltd
12 Avonmouth Road
BR7 8KL Bristol

*4* Petersen Inc
Ogden, UT 84401
324 25th Street

*5* Miss Susan Snow
Smith Street 3
Ipswich IP9 7JH

*6* El Bonito Motel
1710 Mission Bay Drive
CA 92108
San Diego

## 3 Dates

Write out these dates in a correct form for a business letter.

| | | | |
|---|---|---|---|
| *1* 4.5.99 | *3* 01-12-31 | *5* 15.3.01 | *7* 9/6/01 |
| *2* 12.7.2000 | *4* 31/1/99 | *6* 4.8.00 | *8* 00-08-30 |

## 4 A letter of complaint

Pat Norman has just received the delivery of the goods she ordered on 15 September. Unfortunately the consignment was not correct. Put the parts of the letter (A–F) in the correct order. Then write the letter, using the correct layout.

***A*** When we checked the above consignment of wine we found that it was incorrect.

***B*** Dear Mr Fellini

***C*** We have returned twenty bottles of Soave to your address and would be grateful if you could send us the missing 20 bottles of Frascati as soon as possible.

***D*** 28 September 20..

***E*** Instead of the 70 bottles of Soave Cat. No 501 we ordered, we received 90 and instead of the 70 bottles of Frascati Cat. No 581 we ordered, we received only 50.

***F*** Our Order No 1530

# *Pairwork files*

## File 1, Unit 8, Exercise 9

Call Blackwell & Martins to order the following 'Flower Day' sheets (flat, not fitted):

E17231 (size: 180 × 260cm) both in pink
G17233 (size: 270 × 270cm) one in yellow, one in the flowered design

You think the big sheets are £55 each and the small sheets are £40 each.

## File 2, Unit 12, Exercise 12

Student A: First play the part of one of the shop assistants below. Apologize to your customer and help him or her find a solution to the problem. The following notes will help you.

### SHOP ASSISTANT PROFILES

**You work at a greengrocer's.**
Your boss always tells you: If anyone complains about the quality of any fruit or vegetables we have sold, always apologize, give the customer new ones and give him or her a little present as well.

**You sell coats at a department store.**
If the customer has not yet worn the item, exchange it. (But, unfortunately, in this case you have only got other sizes left.) The customer can wait for the new delivery next week or you could give him/her two buttons from another coat.
Remember: Always ask for a receipt when you make an exchange or refund.

Then play the part of a customer and complain about the problems below. (Remember to tell your partner which shop you are in!)

### CUSTOMER PROFILES

**At a sports store**
You would like to exchange a pair of white tennis socks. You washed them in the washing machine at 60 degrees, as it says on the label, but they shrank and now they are too small. You want a new pair or your money back.

**At a department store**
You bought a hair-dryer two months ago. It doesn't work properly any more, only cold air comes out. Take it back to the department store where you bought it. Ask if they can repair it, how much it will cost and how long it will take.

## File 3, Unit 2, Exercise 10

Student B: You are a shop assistant. A customer (student A) asks you for several things. Tell him/her if you have got them or not. Ask how much/many he or she would like.

apples – €1.20 a kilogram

bananas – €1.50 a kilogram

tomatoes – €1.45 a kilogram

muffins – €1.10 each

pretzels – 95 cents each

sandwiches €1.20 each

milk 88 cents a litre

orange juice €1.25 a bottle

mineral water 50 cents a bottle

newspapers 70 cents

## File 4, Unit 8, Exercise 9

Call Blackwell & Martins to order some fitted sheets and the duvet cover for your double bed. (You think you need sheets that are 140 by 200cm and a duvet cover that is 200 by 230cm.) You'd like the bedlinen called 'Flower Day' with the duvet cover in the flowered design and blue or white fitted sheets. You also need two pillowcases in the European size (if they have them). Unfortunately, you don't have the catalogue any more so you don't know the order numbers.

## File 5, Unit 4, Exercise 12

Your partner asks questions about Kevin Davies. Only answer ***yes*** or ***no***.

Kevin Davies lives in a small town near Manchester, England. He is 19 years old and works as a car mechanic. He has a sister, Louisa, who is 12. His mother Miriam, 44, is a cook in a canteen. His father Keith, 43, is a plumber. They have a big aquarium because Kevin likes fish very much. Kevin plays football and he goes to train at the football club three times a week. When he has time he likes reading science fiction books and playing computer games. When Kevin goes to work, he has to get up at quarter past 6 because he's got quite a long way to go. He goes by train for 30 minutes and then by bus for 10 minutes.

## File 6, Unit 8, Exercise 9

You work in the mail-order department at Blackwell & Martins. Use this excerpt from the sales catalogue to take your customer's order.

BEDLINEN

### 30% off *'Flower Day'*

BY SHERIDAN

Bedlinen collection with flower print (yellow, green and pink flowers on blue background) and contrasting plains in 50% cotton, 50% polyester. In print or plain (please specify colour: yellow, green, pink or blue pastel).

| | | | *usual price* | **sale price** |
|---|---|---|---|---|
| ***Flat sheets, each*** | A17597 | 180 × 260cm | £40 | £28 |
| | B17597 | 240 × 260cm | £45 | £31.50 |
| | C17597 | 270 × 270cm | £55 | £38.50 |
| | D17597 | 305 × 270cm | £70 | £49 |
| ***Fitted sheets, each*** | E17597 | 90 × 200cm | £35 | £24.50 |
| | F17597 | 140 × 200cm | £40 | £28 |
| | G17597 | 152 × 203cm | £45 | £31.50 |
| | H17597 | 180 × 203cm | £55 | £38.50 |
| ***Duvet covers, each*** | J17597 | 135 × 220cm | £49 | £34 |
| | K17597 | 200 × 220cm | £69 | £48 |
| | L17597 | 230 × 220cm | £79 | £55 |
| | M17597 | 360 × 220cm | £99 | £69 |
| ***Pillowcases, each*** | S17597 | standard, 48 × 73cm | £10 | £7 |
| | T17597 | European, 65 × 65cm | £18 | £12.50 |

## File 7, Unit 12, Exercise 12

Student B: First play the part of a customer and complain about the problems below. (Remember to tell you partner which shop you are in!)

### CUSTOMER PROFILES

**At a greengrocer's**
You have just bought some onions. When you opened the bag at home, you found that half of them were rotten. Ask for other ones.

**At a department store**
You have just bought a winter coat and at home you find that two buttons are missing. Take the coat back to the department store where you bought it and try to exchange the coat. Don't forget the receipt.

Then play the part of a shop assistant. Apologize to your customer and help him or her find a solution to the problem.

### SHOP ASSISTANT PROFILES

**You work at a sports store.**
Your customer has a problem with a pair of socks that he/she bought on special offer. (The price was very low, so really the customer cannot expect very good quality.) Maybe the customer didn't buy the right size and the socks were too small. Remember: cotton always shrinks in the wash.

**You sell appliances at a department store.**
Before offering to do repairs, check the receipt to make sure the item is still under guarantee. Repairs take about a week. Give the customer the telephone number of your department.

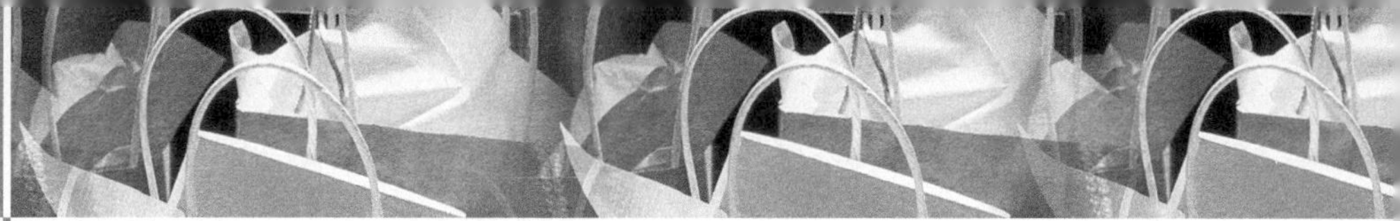

# Transcript

## Unit 1, Exercise 3

My name is Deborah Wood. I'm the manager of SNIPS supermarket. I run the shop and I am often very busy.
Hi, I'm Harry Osborne. I am a shop assistant. I sell cheese and ham at the deli counter.
Hello, I'm Rhaina Panjabi, the window dresser. I come to SNIPS once a week to decorate the shop windows. I like my work here.
My name is Fiona Williams. I'm a cashier. I work on the checkout and take the money from the customers.
Hi, my name is Jason North. I'm one of the trainees. I stock the shelves and sometimes I also work at the deli counter.
I am Beatrice Anderson. I am not a shop assistant, I'm a customer. I come shopping here every day. It's a very good supermarket.

## Unit 2, Exercise 5

*1* The time now is exactly 12.15.
*2* 3 doughnuts are only 1 euro 75 today.
*3* The bill comes to 28 dollars and 65 cents.
*4* We have to pay 122 pounds and 67 pence.
*5* She earns 8,533 pounds a year.
*6* The winning time is 13 minutes and 49 seconds.
*7* We are 14 adults and 40 children, that's 54 altogether.
*8* The distance is 333.4 kilometres.
*9* In this town 71,544 people live in 6,308 buildings.

## Unit 3, Exercise 6

my first job
the second street on your right
the third shelf on your left
the fourth week of April
the fifth month of the year
the sixth aisle
my seventh year at the job
the eighth tin of tomatoes
the ninth trolley in the queue
the tenth bottle of orange juice
my eleventh customer of the day
the twelfth day of the month
my thirteenth birthday

## Unit 3, Exercise 9

MR HAMMON First I need some tinned tomatoes.

EMILY Yes, certainly. How many do you need?

MR HAMMON Six tins. And three tins of peas and … uhm … two chickens.

EMILY Would you like frozen chicken or fresh ones?

MR HAMMON Frozen ones please. And ten juicy apples.

EMILY Yes, I've got that. Anything else?

MR HAMMON Three pineapples, 30 bottles of fizzy mineral water, and have you got washing-up liquid?

EMILY Yes, we have.

MR HAMMON I'd like two please. And then I'd like a large packet of doughnuts and five chocolate muffins.

EMILY Five chocolate muffins. Yes, anything else?

MR HAMMON No, thanks. That's all. What time can you deliver? …

## Unit 4, Exercise 4

This week I have to get up very early. My alarm clock rings at **10 minutes to 5 in the morning**. I work the early shift in our supermarket, so I have to be there at **six o'clock**. That means I have to leave home at **20 minutes past 5**. Our shop doesn't open before **8 o'clock**, but a lot of articles are delivered during the night and we have to store them before we open. Fruit and vegetables are delivered before I arrive, between **5 and half past 5**, the dairy products are delivered between **quarter to 6 and quarter past six**, and bread just before we open, at about **20 minutes to 8**. Then I work at the deli counter for a while. I take a short tea break **around 9** and half an hour's lunch break **between 12 and half past twelve**. I can leave at **3 pm**, and I have the rest of the afternoon off. Sometimes I meet friends in the afternoon or I go to the fitness centre. I go to bed rather early when I'm working the morning shift, at about **half past 9**.

## Unit 5, Exercise 9

*Emily*
I think we should greet customers when they enter the shop. You know, say hello to each person. Then they'll feel bad if they take things from us.

*Harry*
We should all watch our customers all the time. Not just the store detective, but all the cashiers, shop assistants and trainees, too. Then the customers can't take things.

*Jason*
We should stop people from using their own bags or rucksacks. Just tell them they have to use our trolleys.

*Rhaina*
A lot of shoplifters are teenagers. So, put things they like – you know, sweets, soft drinks, cosmetics and videos – near the front of the store. That way we can see what they're doing.

## Unit 6, Exercise 2

(SA = shop assistant; C = customer)

*1*

SA Can I help you, madam?
C Yes, I'd like some grapes, please. Which ones are sweet?
SA Well, these grapes here are very sweet. Would you like to taste one?
C Mmm, good. I'll take that bunch there. And I also need ...

*2*

C Excuse me, I'd like to pick up a pair of glasses.
SA Your name please?
C Wood, Deborah Wood. They're for my daughter. I hope she'll like them.
SA Ah, here they are, Mrs Wood. Now, they look very nice. Your daughter will love them.

*3*

C I'd like some black tights, please.
SA Certainly madam. What's your size?
C Medium.
SA All the ones here are medium.
C I like this pair. How much are they please?

*4*

SA Anything else sir?
C Yes, a packet of these vitamin pills please.
SA Would you like a small packet or a large one?
C How many tablets are in the small one?
SA There are 20 in the small one and 50 in the large one.

## Unit 7, Exercise 8

Let me see. For the starter, I need eight avocados and six tomatoes. Right. I'll get those at the greengrocer's. Oh, and I also need two kilos of potatoes. I'll get those there, too. Mmm ... let's see. I've got that. Ah, then I'll go to the bakery and pick up three loaves of French bread and twelve nut pastries. What else do I need? Oh, yes. I've got to get four more glasses and two knives. I'll get those at ...

## Unit 8, Exercise 5

ALICE Blackwell & Martins Ltd. Good afternoon.
FIONA Good afternoon. My name's Fiona Williams. A friend of mine bought some heart-shaped cushions in your shop some time ago and I wanted to buy some too. But I was away and I didn't have time. Have you still got them?
ALICE Do you know when that was? I'm not quite sure which ones you mean.
FIONA She said she bought them about three weeks ago. They were on the front page of your catalogue.

ALICE Do you mean the bright red velvet ones? I think we have a few left, but could you just hold on a moment, I'll ask my colleague. Hello? No, I'm sorry. We're out of them at the moment. The new delivery didn't arrive on time. But we should get some more tomorrow.

FIONA All right, thank you. I'll call back then. Goodbye.

## Unit 10, Exercise 2

Come to our home textiles department. Hundreds of curtains, towels and tablecloths are now at half price!

A free gift with every pair of inline skates bought – at our sports department on the third floor.

3-piece luggage sets available in three different colours are now 30 per cent reduced – on the third floor.

Visit our cosmetics department on the ground floor – buy any two Giorgio products and get a third one free.

Pure cotton gentlemen's shirts available in different colours and patterns up to 70 per cent off. Men's fashion is on the first floor.

Don't miss the bargains in our household department in the basement: porcelain dinnerware in various designs 30 per cent off the usual prices.

Save up to 50 per cent if you buy a washing machine, dishwasher or microwave oven today in our electrical goods department on the top floor.

## Unit 11, Exercise 8

And here is our next model wearing a lovely casual outfit. The grey and black striped jumper looks perfect with the straight black jeans. Worn with a black leather belt and black shoes, this is a great outfit to wear in the day, and the matching jacket is perfect if the weather gets colder in the evening.

Our next model is wearing a pale blue polyester blouse with a large collar. This smart blouse looks fantastic with a pair of black wool trousers and a matching jacket. The pair of sporty black and white trainers makes this a stylish but relaxed suit, perfect for any office.

# Unit word list

Diese neuen Wörter sind in der Reihenfolge ihres Vorkommens im Text verzeichnet. Es fehlen jedoch die Wörter, die zum Grundwortschatz gehören (siehe Basic Word List).

Die Zahl am linken Rand gibt die Seitenzahl an.
p = das Wort befindet sich im *pairwork file*.
t = das Wort befindet sich im *transcript*.

## Unit 1

6

| | |
|---|---|
| **trainee** [treɪ'niː] | Auszubildende/r, Praktikant/in |
| **supermarket** ['suːpəmɑːkɪt] | Supermarkt |
| **manager** ['mænɪdʒə] | Filialleiter/in, Chef/in |
| **show s.o. round** [ˌʃəʊ 'raʊnd] | jdn herumführen |
| **shop** [ʃɒp] | Laden, Geschäft |
| **introduce** [ˌɪntrə'djuːs] | (sich) vorstellen |
| **a bit** [ə bɪt] | recht, ziemlich |
| **busy** ['bɪzi] | beschäftigt |
| **shop assistant** ['ʃɒp əsɪstənt] | Verkäufer/in |
| **window dresser** ['wɪndəʊ dresə] | Schaufensterdekorateur/in |
| **once** [wʌns] | einmal, wenn einmal |
| **dress** [dres] | dekorieren |
| **shop window** ['ʃɒp wɪndəʊ] | Schaufenster |
| **come on** [ˌkʌm 'ɒn] | beeil dich, los |
| **welcome** ['welkəm] | herzlich willkommen |
| **checkout** ['tʃekaʊt] | Kasse |
| **cashier** [kæ'ʃɪə] | Kassierer/in |
| **guy** [gaɪ] | Kerl, Typ |
| **training** ['treɪnɪŋ] | Ausbildung, Schulung |
| **colleague** ['kɒliːg] | Kollege, Kollegin |
| **box** [bɒks] | Kiste, Karton |
| **of course** [əf 'kɔːs] | natürlich, selbstverständlich |
| **later** ['leɪtə] | später |

7

| | |
|---|---|
| **statement** ['steɪtmənt] | Aussage |
| **question** ['kwestʃən] | Frage |
| **negative** ['negətɪv] | Verneinung; negativ |
| **French** [frentʃ] | französisch; Französisch |
| **introduction** [ˌɪntrə'dʌkʃn] | Vorstellung |
| **partner** ['pɑːtnə] | Partner/in |
| **follow** ['fɒləʊ] | folgen |
| **pleased to meet you** [ˌpliːzd tə 'miːt ju] | Es freut mich, Sie kennen zu lernen. |
| **how do you do** [ˌhaʊ dju 'duː] | Es ist angenehm, Sie kennen zu lernen. |

8

| | |
|---|---|
| **copy** ['kɒpi] | abschreiben, kopieren |
| **table** ['teɪbl] | Tabelle |
| **below** [bɪ'ləʊ] | unten(stehend) |
| **exercise** ['eksəsaɪz] | Übung |
| **listen** ['lɪsn] | zuhören |
| **fill in** [ˌfɪl 'ɪn] | ausfüllen |
| **run** [rʌn] | leiten, führen |

8t

| | |
|---|---|
| **deli counter** ['deli kaʊntə] | Feinkoststand |
| **decorate** ['dekəreɪt] | schmücken, dekorieren |
| **customer** ['kʌstəmə] | Kunde, Kundin |
| **stock** [stɒk] | auffüllen |
| **shelf** [ʃelf] | Regal, Ablage |

8

| | |
|---|---|
| **practice** ['præktɪs] | Übung, Training |
| **full** [fʊl] | voll, vollständig |
| **sentence** ['sentəns] | Satz |
| **example** [ɪg'zɑːmpl] | Beispiel |
| **describe** [dɪ'skraɪb] | beschreiben |
| **rewrite** [ˌriː'raɪt] | umschreiben |
| **correct** [kə'rekt] | richtig, korrekt |
| **form** [fɔːm] | Form; formen |

9

| | |
|---|---|
| **good-looking** [ˌgʊd'lʊkɪŋ] | gut aussehend |
| **university** [ˌjuːnɪ'vɜːsəti] | Universität |
| **assistant** [ə'sɪstənt] | Assistent/in |
| **Austrian** ['ɒstriən] | österreichisch |

10

| | |
|---|---|
| **family tree** [ˌfæməli 'triː] | Stammbaum |
| **complete** [kəm'pliːt] | vervollständigen, ergänzen |
| **text** [tekst] | Text |
| **daughter-in-law** ['dɔːtər ɪn lɔː] | Schwiegertochter |
| **granddaughter** ['grændɔːtə] | Enkelin |
| **find out** [ˌfaɪnd 'aʊt] | herausfinden |
| **grandchildren** ['græntʃɪldrən] | Enkel |
| **married** ['mærid] | verheiratet |
| **just** [dʒʌst] | einfach, nur, bloß, gerade |
| **grandson** ['grænsʌn] | Enkel |
| **nephew** ['nevjuː] | Neffe |
| **niece** [niːs] | Nichte |
| **husband** ['hʌzbənd] | (Ehe-)Mann |
| **mother-in-law** ['mʌðər ɪn lɔː] | Schwiegermutter |

11

| | |
|---|---|
| **hairdresser** ['heədresə] | Friseur, Friseuse |
| **housewife** ['haʊswaɪf] | Hausfrau |
| **gardener** ['gɑːdnə] | Gärtner/in |
| **carpenter** ['kɑːpəntə] | Zimmermann, Tischler/in |
| **nurse** [nɜːs] | Krankenpfleger/in |
| **plumber** ['plʌmə] | Klempner/in |
| **office clerk** ['ɒfɪs klɑːk] | Büroangestellte/r |
| **mechanic** [mɪ'kænɪk] | Mechaniker/in |
| **insurance company** [ɪn'ʃʊərəns kʌmpəni] | Versicherungsgesellschaft |
| **hospital** ['hɒspɪtl] | Krankenhaus |
| **still** [stɪl] | (immer) noch |

| | |
|---|---|
| **be interested in sth** [bi 'ɪntrəstɪd ɪn] | sich interessieren für |
| **woodwork** ['wʊdwɜ:k] | Werken (mit Holz) |
| **install** [ɪn'stɔ:l] | installieren, einbauen |
| **central heating system** [ˌsentrəl 'hi:tɪŋ sɪstəm] | Zentralheizungsanlage |
| **canteen** [kæn'ti:n] | Kantine |
| **repair** [rɪ'peə] | reparieren |
| **retired** [rɪ'taɪəd] | im Ruhestand |
| **own** [əʊn] | eigene/r/s |
| **back garden** [ˌbæk 'gɑ:dn] | Garten (hinter dem Haus) |
| **flower** ['flaʊə] | Blume |
| **plant** [plɑ:nt] | Pflanze |
| **draw** [drɔ:] | zeichnen |
| **puzzle** ['pʌzl] | Rätsel |
| **onto** ['ɒntə] | auf |
| **separate** ['seprət] | andere/r/s |
| **piece** [pi:s] | Stück, Blatt |
| **member** ['membə] | Mitglied |

## Unit 2

| | |
|---|---|
| 12 | |
| **grocery shop** ['grəʊsəri ʃɒp] | Lebensmittelgeschäft |
| **pretzel** ['pretsl] | Brezel |
| **certainly** ['sɜ:tnli] | sicher, gerne |
| **anything else** ['enɪθɪŋ els] | sonst noch etwas |
| **bottle** ['bɒtl] | Flasche |
| **litre** ['li:tə] | Liter |
| **here you are** [hɪə ju 'ɑ:] | bitte |
| 13 | |
| **American** [ə'merɪkən] | Amerikaner/in |
| **Briton** ['brɪtn] | Brite/Britin |
| **Spanish** ['spænɪʃ] | spanisch |
| 14 | |
| **match** [mætʃ] | zuordnen, (zusammen) passen |
| **get up** [ˌget 'ʌp] | aufstehen |
| **doughnut** ['dəʊnʌt] | Krapfen, Pfannkuchen |
| **coin** [kɔɪn] | Münze |
| **sunshine** ['sʌnʃaɪn] | Sonnenschein |
| **rain** [reɪn] | Regen |
| **teacup** ['ti:kʌp] | Teetasse |
| **tea** [ti:] | Tee |
| **juice** [dʒu:s] | Saft |
| **cost** [kɒst] | Kosten; kosten |
| **carrot** ['kærət] | Karotte, Möhre |
| 15 | |
| **cardinal number** [ˌkɑ:dɪnl 'nʌmbə] | Kardinalzahl |
| **hear** [hɪə] | hören |
| 15t | |
| **exactly** [ɪg'zæktli] | genau |
| **bill** [bɪl] | Rechnung |
| **earn** [ɜ:n] | verdienen |
| **win** [wɪn] | gewinnen, siegen |
| **altogether** [ˌɔ:ltə'geðə] | insgesamt, im Ganzen |
| **distance** ['dɪstəns] | Entfernung, Abstand |
| **building** ['bɪldɪŋ] | Gebäude |
| 15 | |
| **sandwich** ['sænwɪdʒ] | Sandwich |
| **bunch** [bʌntʃ] | Bund |
| **muffin** ['mʌfɪn] | Muffin |
| 16 | |
| **pair** [peə] | Paar |
| **manage** ['mænɪdʒ] | (es) schaffen |
| **change** [tʃeɪndʒ] | Wechselgeld, Kleingeld |
| **receipt** [rɪ'si:t] | Quittung, Beleg |
| **note** [nəʊt] | Note, Schein |
| **polite** [pə'laɪt] | höflich |
| 17 | |
| **item** ['aɪtəm] | Artikel, Gegenstand, Ding |
| **such as** ['sʌtʃ əz] | wie zum Beispiel |
| **etc** [ˌet 'setərə] | usw. |
| **role play** ['rəʊl pleɪ] | Rollenspiel |
| **student** ['stju:dnt] | Schüler/in, Student/in |
| **file** [faɪl] | Akte |
| **both** [bəʊθ] | beide |
| 17p | |
| **several** ['sevrəl] | einige, mehrere |

## Unit 3

| | |
|---|---|
| 18 | |
| **entrance** ['entrəns] | Eingang |
| **trolley** ['trɒli] | (Einkaufs-)Wagen |
| **exit** ['eksɪt] | Ausgang |
| **biscuit** ['bɪskɪt] | Keks |
| **pasta** ['pæstə] | Nudeln |
| **flour** ['flaʊə] | Mehl |
| **jam** [dʒæm] | Marmelade, Konfitüre |
| **honey** ['hʌni] | Honig |
| **spirits** ['spɪrɪts] | Spirituosen |
| **soft drinks** [ˌsɒft 'drɪŋks] | alkoholfreie Getränke |
| **frozen food** [ˌfrəʊzn 'fu:d] | Tiefkühlkost |
| **spices** ['spaɪsɪz] | Gewürze |
| **dairy products** ['deəri prɒdʌkts] | Milchprodukte |
| **pet food** ['pet fu:d] | Tierfutter |
| **toilet paper** ['tɔɪlət peɪpə] | Toilettenpapier |
| **washing powder** ['wɒʃɪŋ paʊdə] | Waschpulver |
| **household cleaning products** [ˌhaʊshəʊld 'kli:nɪŋ prɒdʌkts] | Haushaltsreiniger |
| **mustard** ['mʌstəd] | Senf |
| **meat** [mi:t] | Fleisch |
| **sausage** ['sɒsɪdʒ] | Wurst |
| **poultry** ['pəʊltri] | Geflügel |
| 19 | |
| **choose** [tʃu:z] | wählen, aussuchen |
| **straight ahead** [ˌstreɪt ə'hed] | geradeaus |
| **corner** ['kɔ:nə] | Ecke |
| **aisle** [aɪl] | Gang |
| **behind** [bɪ'haɪnd] | hinter, hinten |
| **between** [bɪ'twi:n] | zwischen |
| **in front of** [ɪn 'frʌnt əv] | vor |
| **opposite** ['ɒpəzɪt] | gegenüber(liegend) |
| **turn** [tɜ:n] | abbiegen, (sich) umdrehen |
| **make up** [ˌmeɪk 'ʌp] | erfinden, sich ausdenken |
| **similar** ['sɪmələ] | ähnlich |
| **cat food** ['kæt fu:d] | Katzenfutter |
| 20 | |
| **belong to** [bɪ'lɒŋ tə] | (dazu) gehören, angehören |
| **afraid, I'm ~** [ə'freɪd] | leider |
| **wrong** [rɒŋ] | unrecht haben |
| **shopping bag** ['ʃɒpɪŋ bæg] | Einkaufstasche |

21
**machine** [mə'ʃi:n] Maschine, Gerät
**clean** [kli:n] reinigen
**save** [seɪv] sparen
**type** [taɪp] tippen
**fix** [fɪks] reparieren
**garage** ['gærɑ:ʒ] (Auto-)Werkstatt
**ordinal number** [ˌɔ:dɪnl 'nʌmbə] Ordnungszahl
**tin** [tɪn] Dose

21t
**queue** [kju:] Schlange

22
**bacon** ['beɪkən] Schinkenspeck
**beans** [bi:nz] Bohnen
**cauliflower** [kɒliflaʊə] Blumenkohl
**chicken** ['tʃɪkɪn] Huhn, Hähnchen
**lobster** ['lɒbstə] Hummer
**fizzy** ['fɪzi] sprudelnd
**nutmeg** ['nʌtmeg] Muskat
**parsley** ['pɑ:sli] Petersilie
**pineapple** ['paɪnæpl] Ananas
**sardine** [ˌsɑ:'di:n] Sardine
**strawberry** ['strɔ:bəri] Erdbeere
**washing-up liquid** [ˌwɒʃɪŋ'ʌp lɪkwɪd] Spülmittel
**dictionary** ['dɪkʃənri] Wörterbuch
**add** [æd] hinzufügen
**herbs** [hɜ:bz] Kräuter
**drink** [drɪŋk] Getränk
**seafood** ['si:fu:d] Meeresfrüchte
**cosmetics** [kɒz'metɪks] Kosmetik(a)
**personal hygiene articles** [ˌpɜ:sənl ˌhaɪdʒi:n 'ɑ:tɪklz] Toilettenartikel
**detergents** [dɪ'tɜ:dʒənts] Reinigungsmittel, Waschmittel
**cleaning products** ['kli:nɪŋ prɒdʌkts] Putzmittel

23
**shopping list** ['ʃɒpɪŋ lɪst] Einkaufsliste
**deliver** [dɪ'lɪvə] liefern
**office** ['ɒfɪs] Amt, Büro
**mistake** [mɪ'steɪk] Fehler
**fresh** [freʃ] frisch
**packet** ['pækɪt] Päckchen, Paket
**nut** [nʌt] Nuss

23t
**tinned** [tɪnd] Dosen-, Büchsen-
**pea** [pi:] Erbse
**frozen** ['frəʊzn] (tief)gefroren
**juicy** ['dʒu:si] saftig

23
**mean** [mi:n] bedeuten
**important** [ɪm'pɔ:tnt] wichtig
**careful** ['keəfl] vorsichtig
**mark** [mɑ:k] Zeichen
**store** [stɔ:] lagern
**fridge** [frɪdʒ] Kühlschrank
**best before date** [best bɪ'fɔ: deɪt] Verfallsdatum
**handle** ['hændl] anfassen, berühren
**cracked** [krækt] angestoßen
**dirty** ['dɜ:ti] schmutzig
**raw** [rɔ:] roh
**lightly** ['laɪtli] leicht
**pregnant** ['pregnənt] schwanger
**vulnerable** ['vʌlnərəbl] verletzbar

## Unit 4

24
**pen-friend** ['penfrend] Brieffreund/in
**advertisement (ad)** [əd'vɜ:tɪsmənt, æd] Anzeige
**exchange** [ɪks'tʃeɪndʒ] austauschen
**together** [tə'geðə] zusammen
**divorced** [dɪ'vɔ:st] geschieden
**tabby** ['tæbi] getigerte Katze
**pet** [pet] Haustier
**hours** ['aʊəz] Arbeitszeit
**am** [ˌeɪ 'em] vor 12 Uhr
**till, until** [tɪl, ən'tɪl] bis
**pm** [ˌpi: 'em] nach 12 Uhr
**twice** [twaɪs] zweimal
**off** [ɒf] frei
**spare** [speə] übrig haben
**kind** [kaɪnd] Art
**favourite** ['feɪvərɪt] Lieblings-
**look forward to** [ˌlʊk 'fɔ:wəd tə] sich freuen auf
**best wishes** [best 'wɪʃɪz] Viele Grüße, Alles Gute
**guitar** [gɪ'tɑ:] Gitarre
**computer game** [kəm'pju:tə geɪm] Computerspiel
**Hungarian** [hʌŋ'geəriən] Ungarisch
**sailing** ['seɪlɪŋ] Segeln
**cycling** ['saɪklɪŋ] Radfahren
**singer** ['sɪŋə] Sänger/in
**band** [bænd] (Musik-)Kapelle
**fifties** ['fɪftiz] Fünfziger
**sixties** ['sɪkstiz] Sechziger
**Italian** [ɪ'tæljən] Italienisch
**skiing** ['ski:ɪŋ] Skilaufen
**surfing** ['sɜ:fɪŋ] Surfing
**motorbike** ['məʊtəbaɪk] Motorrad
**Turkish** ['tɜ:kɪʃ] Türkisch

25
**true** [tru:] richtig
**false** [fɔ:ls] falsch
**past** [pɑ:st] nach
**quarter** ['kwɔ:tə] Viertel

26
**catch** [kætʃ] erreichen, nehmen
**lunch break** ['lʌntʃ breɪk] Mittagspause
**shift** [ʃɪft] Schicht
**notes** [nəʊts] Notizen
**alarm clock** [ə'lɑ:m klɒk] Wecker
**ring** [rɪŋ] klingeln, läuten

26t
**article** ['ɑ:tɪkl] Artikel, Gegenstand
**during** ['djʊərɪŋ] während
**while** [waɪl] Weile
**tea break** ['ti: breɪk] Teepause
**rest** [rest] Rest
**fitness centre** ['fɪtnəs sentə] Fitnesscenter
**rather** ['rɑ:ðə] ziemlich

27
**daily** ['deɪli] täglich, Tages-
**routine** [ru:'ti:n] Routine

| | |
|---|---|
| **usually** ['ju:ʒuəli] | normalerweise, gewöhnlich |
| **lunch** [lʌntʃ] | Mittagessen |
| **underground** ['ʌndəgraʊnd] | U-Bahn |

28

| | |
|---|---|
| **go out** [ˌgəʊ 'aʊt] | ausgehen |
| **certain** ['sɜ:tn] | sicher, gewiss, bestimmt |
| **hate** [heɪt] | hassen, gar nicht mögen |
| **translation** [træns'leɪʃn] | Übersetzung |
| **translate** [træns'leɪt] | übersetzen |
| **check** [tʃek] | kontrollieren, (über)prüfen |

29

| | |
|---|---|
| **hardly ever** [ˌhɑ:dli 'evə] | fast nie |
| **phrase** [freɪz] | Redewendung |
| **times** [taɪmz] | mal |

30

| | |
|---|---|
| **try** [traɪ] | versuchen |
| **possible** ['pɒsəbl] | möglich |

30p

| | |
|---|---|
| **aquarium** [ə'kweəriəm] | Aquarium |
| **train** [treɪn] | trainieren |
| **science fiction** [ˌsaɪəns 'fɪkʃn] | Sciencefiction |
| **quite** [kwaɪt] | ziemlich, ganz |
| **a long way** [ə lɒŋ 'weɪ] | ein weiter Weg |
| **reply** [rɪ'plaɪ] | antworten |
| **season** ['si:zn] | Jahreszeit |

## Unit 5

31

| | |
|---|---|
| **ideal** [aɪ'di:əl] | ideal |
| **shopper** ['ʃɒpə] | Käufer/in |
| **identify** [aɪ'dentɪfaɪ] | erkennen |
| **goods** [gʊdz] | Ware(n) |
| **special offer** [ˌspeʃl 'ɒfə] | Sonderangebot |
| **household budget** [ˌhaʊshəʊld 'bʌdʒɪt] | Haushaltskasse |
| **healthy** ['helθi] | gesund |
| **organically grown** [ɔ:'gænɪkli grəʊn] | organisch angebaut |
| **free range** [ˌfri:'reɪndʒ] | Freiland- |
| **compare** [kəm'peə] | vergleichen |
| **different** ['dɪfrənt] | verschieden |
| **sensible** ['sensəbl] | vernünftig |
| **decision** [dɪ'sɪʒn] | Entscheidung |
| **reduced** [rɪ'dju:st] | reduziert |
| **package** ['pækɪdʒ] | Paket, Verpackung |
| **habit** ['hæbɪt] | Gewohnheit |
| **plan** [plæn] | planen |
| **meal** [mi:l] | Essen |
| **hectic** ['hektɪk] | hektisch |
| **quickly** ['kwɪkli] | schnell, rasch |
| **impulse** ['ɪmpʌls] | Impuls |
| **even if** ['i:vn ɪf] | selbst wenn |
| **idealist** [aɪ'di:əlɪst] | Idealist |
| **organic** [ɔ:'gænɪk] | organisch |
| **environmentally friendly** [ɪnˌvaɪrənˌmentəli 'frendli] | umweltfreundlich |
| **product** ['prɒdʌkt] | Produkt |
| **too** [tu:] | zu |
| **packaging** ['pækɪdʒɪŋ] | Verpackung |
| **strange** [streɪndʒ] | seltsam |

32

| | |
|---|---|
| **agree** [ə'gri:] | übereinstimmen |
| **disagree** [ˌdɪsə'gri:] | nicht übereinstimmen |
| **opinion** [ə'pɪniən] | Meinung |
| **seem** [si:m] | (er)scheinen |
| **enjoy** [ɪn'dʒɔɪ] | genießen, gern haben/tun |
| **probably** ['prɒbəbli] | wahrscheinlich |
| **believe** [bɪ'li:v] | glauben |
| **terribly** ['terəbli] | furchtbar |
| **hardly** ['hɑ:dli] | kaum |
| **lately** ['leɪtli] | in letzter Zeit |

33

| | |
|---|---|
| **badly** ['bædli] | sehr, schlecht |
| **completely** [kəm'pli:tli] | völlig |
| **directly** [də'rektli] | direkt |
| **properly** ['prɒpəli] | richtig, korrekt |
| **product line** ['prɒdʌkt laɪn] | Produktlinie |
| **empty** ['empti] | leer |
| **damaged** ['dæmɪdʒd] | beschädigt |
| **calculator** ['kælkjuleɪtə] | Taschenrechner |
| **sensibly** ['sensəbli] | vernünftig |
| **exact** [ɪg'zækt] | genau |
| **quick** [kwɪk] | schnell |
| **shortly** ['ʃɔ:tli] | kurz |
| **watch** [wɒtʃ] | beobachten |
| **carefully** ['keəfəli] | sorgfältig |

34

| | |
|---|---|
| **monitor** ['mɒnɪtə] | Monitor |
| **enter** ['entə] | hineingehen, betreten |
| **jar** [dʒɑ:] | Glas |

35

| | |
|---|---|
| **drive** [draɪv] | (Auto)fahren |
| **work** [wɜ:k] | funktionieren, arbeiten |
| **cash** [kæʃ] | Bargeld |
| **simple** ['sɪmpl] | einfach |
| **flat** [flæt] | Wohnung |
| **France** [frɑ:ns] | Frankreich |
| **shoplifter** ['ʃɒplɪftə] | Ladendieb/in |
| **happen** ['hæpən] | passieren |

36

| | |
|---|---|
| **steal** [sti:l] | stehlen |

36t

| | |
|---|---|
| **greet** [gri:t] | (be)grüßen |
| **store detective** [ˌstɔ: dɪ'tektɪv] | Hausdetektiv |
| **rucksack** ['rʌksæk] | Rucksack |

36

| | |
|---|---|
| **fill** [fɪl] | füllen |
| **gap** [gæp] | Lücke |

## Unit 6

37

| | |
|---|---|
| **bakery** ['beɪkəri] | Bäckerei |
| **grocer** ['grəʊsə] | Lebensmittelhändler/in |
| **florist** ['flɒrɪst] | Blumenhändler/in |
| **household electronics** [ˌhaʊshəʊld ˌɪlek'trɒnɪks] | Haushaltselektronik |
| **hardware** ['hɑ:dweə] | Eisenwaren, Haushaltswaren |
| **optician** [ɒp'tɪʃn] | Optiker/in |
| **news agent** ['nju:z eɪdʒənt] | Zeitungshändler |
| **butcher** ['bʊtʃə] | Fleischer/in |
| **fashion boutique** [ˌfæʃn bu:'ti:k] | Modeboutique |
| **chemist** ['kemɪst] | Apotheke |

| | |
|---|---|
| **jeweller** ['dʒu:ələ] | Juwelier/in |
| **shoe shop** ['ʃu: ʃɒp] | Schuhgeschäft |
| **sports shop** ['spɔ:ts ʃɒp] | Sportgeschäft |

37t

| | |
|---|---|
| **grape** [greɪp] | Weintraube |
| **taste** [teɪst] | kosten, probieren |
| **pick up** [ˌpɪk 'ʌp] | abholen |
| **tights** [taɪts] | (eine) Strumpfhose |
| **size** [saɪz] | Größe |
| **vitamin** ['vɪtəmɪn] | Vitamin |
| **pill** [pɪl] | Pille |
| **tablet** ['tæblɪt] | Tablette |

38

| | |
|---|---|
| **dozen** ['dʌzn] | Dutzend |
| **pork** [pɔ:k] | Schweinefleisch |
| **bar of chocolate** [bɑ:r əv 'tʃɒklət] | Tafel Schokolade |
| **contact lens cleaner** [ˌkɒntækt lenz 'kli:nə] | Kontaktlinsenreiniger |
| **lighter** ['laɪtə] | Feuerzeug |
| **rose** [rəʊz] | Rose |
| **iron** ['aɪən] | Bügeleisen |
| **head of lettuce** [ˌhed əv 'letɪs] | Salatkopf |
| **loaf** [ləʊf] | Laib |
| **wholemeal** ['həʊlmi:l] | Vollkorn- |
| **painkiller** ['peɪnkɪlə] | schmerzstillendes Mittel |
| **sunglasses** ['sʌnglɑ:sɪz] | Sonnenbrille |
| **tube** [tju:b] | Tube |
| **glue** [glu:] | Klebstoff |
| **shoe polish** ['ʃu: pɒlɪʃ] | Schuhcreme |
| **tub** [tʌb] | Becher |
| **margarine** [ˌmɑ:dʒə'ri:n] | Margarine |
| **toothpaste** ['tu:θpeɪst] | Zahnpasta |
| **tour** [tʊə] | Tour |
| **through** [θru:] | durch … hindurch, durch |
| **finally** ['faɪnəli] | schließlich, zum Schluss |

39

| | |
|---|---|
| **express** [ɪk'spres] | ausdrücken |
| **few** [fju:] | ein paar, wenige |
| **peanut** ['pi:nʌt] | Erdnuss |
| **couple** ['kʌpl] | ein paar, einige |
| **trousers** ['traʊzəz] | Hose |

40

| | |
|---|---|
| **expression** [ɪk'spreʃn] | Ausdruck |
| **slice** [slaɪs] | Scheibe |
| **vinegar** ['vɪnɪgə] | Essig |
| **poor** [pʊə] | schlecht, mangelhaft |
| **variety** [və'raɪəti] | Vielfalt, Auswahl |
| **prefer** [prɪ'fɜ:] | lieber mögen |
| **rye** [raɪ] | Roggen |
| **mainly** ['meɪnli] | hauptsächlich, vor allem |
| **wheat** [wi:t] | Weizen |
| **contain** [kən'teɪn] | enthalten |
| **linseed** ['lɪnsi:d] | Leinsamen |
| **poppy seed** ['pɒpi si:d] | Mohn(samen) |
| **sunflower seed** ['sʌnflaʊə si:d] | Sonnenblumenkerne |
| **pumpkin seed** ['pʌmpkɪn si:d] | Kürbiskerne |
| **olive** ['ɒlɪv] | Olive |
| **walnut** ['wɔ:lnʌt] | Walnuss |
| **sound** [saʊnd] | (sich) anhören, klingen |
| **delicious** [dɪ'lɪʃəs] | köstlich, lecker |
| **pastry** ['peɪstri] | Gebäck |
| **filled with** ['fɪld wɪð] | gefüllt mit |
| **apple strudel** [ˌæpl 'stru:dl] | Apfelstrudel |
| **cinnamon** ['sɪnəmən] | Zimt |
| **vanilla custard** [və'nɪlə kʌstəd] | Vanillesoße |
| **apricot** ['eɪprɪkɒt] | Aprikose |
| **carrier bag** ['kæriə bæg] | Tragetüte |

41

| | |
|---|---|
| **Italy** ['ɪtəli] | Italien |
| **melon** ['melən] | Melone |
| **new potato** [nju: pə'teɪtəʊ] | Frühkartoffel |

42

| | |
|---|---|
| **watch** [wɒtʃ] | (Armband-)Uhr |
| **pot plant** ['pɒt plɑ:nt] | Topfpflanze |
| **racket** ['rækɪt] | Schläger |

43

| | |
|---|---|
| **spinach** ['spɪnɪtʃ] | Spinat |
| **freezer** ['fri:zə] | Gefrierschrank, Tiefkühltruhe |
| **sales** [seɪlz] | Verkaufs- |
| **act out** [ækt] | durchspielen |

## Unit 7

44

| | |
|---|---|
| **foreign** ['fɒrən] | Auslands-, ausländisch |
| **visitor** ['vɪzɪtə] | Besucher/in, Gast |
| **stay** [steɪ] | bleiben, übernachten |
| **menu** ['menju:] | Speisekarte, Menü |
| **sure** [ʃʊə] | sicher |
| **sautée** ['səʊteɪ] | (kurz) anbraten |
| **mushroom** ['mʌʃrʊm] | Pilz, Champignon |
| **fry** [fraɪ] | braten, frittieren |
| **pan** [pæn] | Pfanne |
| **sponge pudding** [ˌspʌndʒ 'pʊdɪŋ] | Biskuitpudding |
| **light** [laɪt] | leicht |
| **traditional** [trə'dɪʃənl] | traditionell |
| **dessert** [dɪ'zɜ:t] | Nachspeise, Dessert |
| **cheesecake** ['tʃi:zkeɪk] | Käsekuchen |
| **blackberry** ['blækbəri] | Brombeere |
| **crumble** ['krʌmbl] | mit Streusel |
| **crumbly** ['krʌmbli] | krümelig |
| **topping** ['tɒpɪŋ] | Belag |
| **maybe** ['meɪbi] | vielleicht |
| **main course** [ˌmeɪn 'kɔ:s] | Hauptgericht |
| **dish** [dɪʃ] | Gericht |
| **chips** [tʃɪps] | Pommes frites |
| **batter** ['bætə] | Eierteig |
| **mixture** ['mɪkstʃə] | Mischung |
| **fillet** ['fɪlɪt] | Filet |
| **garlic** ['gɑ:lɪk] | Knoblauch |
| **cola** ['kəʊlə] | Cola |

45

| | |
|---|---|
| **cheers** [tʃɪəz] | Prost! |

46

| | |
|---|---|
| **starter** ['stɑ:tə] | Vorspeise |
| **serve** [sɜ:v] | servieren, bedienen |
| **chicken wings** ['tʃɪkɪn wɪŋz] | Hähnchenflügel |
| **spicy** ['spaɪsi] | (stark) gewürzt, scharf |
| **barbecue sauce** ['bɑ:bɪkju: sɔ:s] | Grillsauce |
| **tiger prawn** ['taɪgə prɔ:n] | Krabbe |
| **chilli** ['tʃɪli] | Chili |
| **dip** [dɪp] | Dip |
| **forest fruits** ['fɒrɪst fru:ts] | Waldfrüchte |

**garnish** ['gɑ:nɪʃ] garnieren
**duck** [dʌk] Ente
**paté** ['pæteɪ] Pastete
**redcurrant jelly** [red 'kʌrənt dʒeli] rotes Johannisbeergelee
**buttered** ['bʌtəd] mit Butter bestrichen
**side order** ['saɪd ɔ:də] Beilage
**onion ring** ['ʌnjən rɪŋ] Zwiebelring
**garlic bread** ['gɑ:lɪk bred] Knoblauchbrot
**portion** ['pɔ:ʃn] Portion
**side salad** [ˌsaɪd 'sæləd] Salat (als Beilage)
**breast** [brest] Brust
**herb** [hɜ:b] (Würz)Kraut
**roast** [rəʊst] Braten; braten
**pepper** ['pepə] Paprika(schote)
**layer** ['leɪə] Schicht
**cod** [kɒd] Kabeljau
**prawn** [prɔ:n] Garnele, Krabbe
**creamy** ['kri:mi] sahnig
**top with** ['tɒp wɪð] belegen mit
**avocado** [ˌævə'kɑ:dəʊ] Avocado
**sweetcorn** [kɔ:n] Mais
**bake** [beɪk] backen
**golden** ['gəʊldən] golden
**coq au vin** [ˌkɒk əʊ 'væn] Hähnchen in Weinsoße
**rich** [rɪtʃ] schwer
**wild rice** [ˌwaɪld 'raɪs] Wildreis
**sirloin steak** ['sɜ:lɔɪn steɪk] Filetsteak
**tender** ['tendə] zart
**beef** [bi:f] Rindfleisch
**grill** [grɪl] grillen
**liking** ['laɪkɪŋ] Geschmack
**speciality** [ˌspeʃi'æləti] Spezialität
**mash** [mæʃ] Kartoffelpüree
**mashed** [mæʃt] püriert
**onion** ['ʌnjən] Zwiebel
**gravy** ['greɪvi] Soße
**choice** [tʃɔɪs] Wahl, Auswahl
**custard** ['kʌstəd] Vanillesoße
**double** ['dʌbl] Doppel-
**mousse** [mu:s] Creme
**cheese and biscuits** [ˌtʃi:z ənd 'bɪskɪts] Käse und Kekse
**crispy** ['krɪspi] knusprig
**selection** [sɪ'lekʃn] Auswahl
**beverage** ['bevərɪdʒ] Getränk
**pot** [pɒt] Kanne
**include** [ɪn'klu:d] inklusive
**service charge** ['sɜ:vɪs tʃɑ:dʒ] Bedienungsgeld
**VAT** [ˌvi: eɪ 'ti:] MWSt

47
**waitress** ['weɪtrɪs] Kellnerin
**waiter** ['weɪtə] Kellner
**care for** ['keə fə] gerne haben
**rare** [reə] halb roh
**well done** [ˌwel 'dʌn] gut durchgebraten
**teach** [ti:tʃ] beibringen
**difficult** ['dɪfɪkəlt] schwer, schwierig
**tricky** ['trɪki] knifflig, schwierig
**related** [rɪ'leɪtɪd] verwandt
**continue** [kən'tɪnju:] (sich) fortsetzen, fortfahren
**conversation** [ˌkɒnvə'seɪʃn] Gespräch

49
**explain** [ɪk'spleɪn] erklären
**dumpling** ['dʌmplɪŋ] Knödel
**boil** [bɔɪl] kochen
**stew** [stju:] Eintopf(gericht); schmoren
**ingredient** [ɪn'gri:diənt] Zutat
**cabbage** ['kæbɪdʒ] Kohl
**leek** [li:k] Porree
**plaice** [pleɪs] Scholle
**liver** ['lɪvə] Leber
**veal** [vi:l] Kalbfleisch
**chop** [tʃɒp] Kotelett
**style** [staɪl] Stil
**term** [tɜ:m] Ausdruck
**deep fry** [ˌdi:p 'fraɪ] in Fett backen
**Chinese** [tʃaɪ'ni:z] chinesisch
**cuisine** [kwɪ'zi:n] Küche
**Indian** ['ɪndiən] indisch
**famous** ['feɪməs] berühmt
**cooker** ['kʊkə] Herd
**desert** ['dezət] Wüste

50
**recipe** ['resəpi] (Koch-)Rezept
**instruction** [ɪn'strʌkʃn] Anweisung
**roll** [rəʊl] Brötchen
**tablespoon** ['teɪblspu:n] Esslöffel
**sprinkle** ['sprɪŋkl] streuen
**mix** [mɪks] mischen
**cube** [kju:b] Würfel
**bowl** [bəʊl] Schüssel
**finely** ['faɪnli] dünn
**done** [dʌn] gar
**cut** [kʌt] (zer-/durch)schneiden
**pour** [pɔ:] gießen
**spoon** [spu:n] Löffel
**side dish** ['saɪd dɪʃ] Beilage
**safe** [seɪf] Safe, Tresor
**roof** [ru:f] Dach
**knife** [naɪf] Messer
**sheep** [ʃi:p] Schaf
**dinner party** ['dɪnə pɑ:ti] Abendgesellschaft
**attention** [ə'tenʃn] Aufmerksamkeit

## Unit 8

51
**message** ['mesɪdʒ] Nachricht
**reach** [ri:tʃ] erreichen
**mobile phone** [ˌməʊbaɪl 'fəʊn] Handy
**soon** [su:n] bald
**ago** [ə'gəʊ] vor
**ring so back** [ˌrɪŋ 'bæk] jdn zurückrufen

52
**bedlinen** ['bedlɪnɪn] Bettwäsche
**linen** ['lɪnɪn] Leinen
**Ltd** ['lɪmɪtɪd] GmbH
**sale** [seɪl] Verkauf
**catalogue** ['kætəlɒg] Katalog
**put s.o. through** [ˌpʊt 'θru:] jdn verbinden
**mail-order** [ˌmeɪl 'ɔ:də] Postversand
**department** [dɪ'pɑ:tmənt] Abteilung
**pause** [pɔ:z] Pause
**extension** [ɪk'stenʃn] Apparat, Durchwahl
**engaged** [ɪn'geɪdʒd] besetzt
**duvet cover** ['du:veɪ kʌvə] Tagesdecke
**pillowcase** ['pɪləʊkeɪs] Kopfkissenbezug
**standard** ['stændəd] Normal
**repeat** [rɪ'pi:t] wiederholen

| | |
|---|---|
| **spell** [spel] | buchstabieren |
| **send** [send] | schicken |
| **within** [wɪ'ðɪn] | innerhalb (von), in |
| **all right** [ɔ:l 'raɪt] | in Ordnung, (schon) gut |

53

| | |
|---|---|
| **surname** ['sɜ:neɪm] | Nach-, Familienname |

54

| | |
|---|---|
| **velvet** ['velvɪt] | Samt |
| **heart shaped** ['hɑ:tʃeɪpt] | herzförmig |
| **cushion** ['kʊʃn] | Kissen |
| **quiet** ['kwaɪət] | ruhig, leise |
| **bright** [braɪt] | leuchtend, hell |
| **left** [left] | übrig |
| **delivery** [dɪ'lɪvəri] | Lieferung |
| **material** [mə'tɪəriəl] | Stoff |
| **hold on** [ˌhəʊld 'ɒn] | bleiben Sie dran |
| **available** [ə'veɪləbl] | erhältlich |

54t

| | |
|---|---|
| **be away** [bi ə'weɪ] | weg sein |
| **out of sth** ['aʊt əv] | kein mehr haben |

55

| | |
|---|---|
| **sports shoes** ['spɔ:ts ʃu:z] | Sportschuhe |
| **actually** ['æktʃuəli] | eigentlich |
| **decide** [dɪ'saɪd] | (sich) entscheiden |
| **fine** [faɪn] | schön |
| **pub** [pʌb] | Kneipe |

56

| | |
|---|---|
| **diary** ['daɪəri] | Terminkalender |
| **musical** ['mju:zɪkl] | Musical |
| **feed** [fi:d] | füttern |
| **airport** ['eəpɔ:t] | Flughafen |
| **urgent** ['ɜ:dʒənt] | dringend |
| **keep s.o. waiting** [ki:p 'weɪtɪŋ] | jdn warten lassen |
| **direct** [də'rekt] | direkt |
| **mind** [maɪnd] | etw dagegen haben |
| **get in touch** [get ɪn 'tʌtʃ] | (sich) in Verbindung setzen |
| **dial** ['daɪəl] | wählen |
| **excerpt** ['eksɜ:pt] | Auszug |
| **profile** ['prəʊfaɪl] | Profil, Beschreibung |

56p

| | |
|---|---|
| **off, 30% ~** [ɒf] | Nachlass (von 30%) |
| **collection** [kə'lekʃn] | Kollektion |
| **print** [prɪnt] | Muster |
| **background** ['bækgraʊnd] | Hintergrund |
| **contrasting** [kən'trɑ:stɪŋ] | kontrastrierend |
| **plain** [pleɪn] | einfarbig |
| **cotton** ['kɒtn] | Baumwolle |
| **polyester** [ˌpɒli'estə] | Polyester |
| **specify** ['spesɪfaɪ] | aufführen, spezifizieren |
| **pastel** ['pæstl] | pastellfarben |
| **usual** ['ju:ʒuəl] | gewöhnlich |
| **flat sheet** [flæt 'ʃi:t] | Bettuch |
| **fitted sheet** [ˌfɪtɪd 'ʃi:t] | Spannbettuch |
| **flowered** ['flaʊəd] | geblümt |
| **design** [dɪ'zaɪn] | Muster |
| **unfortunately** [ʌn'fɔ:tʃənətli] | leider |
| **any more** [eni 'mɔ:] | nicht ... mehr |

## Unit 9

57

| | |
|---|---|
| **souvenir** [ˌsu:və'nɪə] | Andenken |
| **abroad** [ə'brɔ:d] | im Ausland |
| **fragile** ['frædʒaɪl] | zerbrechlich |
| **pretty** ['prɪti] | hübsch |
| **depend on** [dɪ'pend ɒn] | abhängen von |
| **elephant** ['elɪfənt] | Elefant |
| **owl** [aʊl] | Eule |
| **cheap** [tʃi:p] | billig |
| **expensive** [ɪk'spensɪv] | teuer |
| **ordinary** ['ɔ:dnri] | gewöhnlich |
| **lead crystal** [led 'krɪstl] | Bleikristall |
| **brand** [brænd] | Marke |
| **best selling** [ˌbest 'selɪŋ] | absatzstark |
| **assistance** [ə'sɪstəns] | Hilfe |
| **feature** ['fi:tʃə] | Merkmal |

58

| | |
|---|---|
| **cuckoo clock** ['kʊku: klɒk] | Kuckucksuhr |
| **hand** [hænd] | Zeiger |
| **clock-face** ['klɒkfeɪs] | Zifferblatt |
| **cuckoo** ['kʊku:] | Kuckuck |
| **battery** ['bætəri] | Batterie |
| **inside** ['ɪnsaɪd] | innen |
| **battery operated** ['bætəri ɒpəreɪtɪd] | batteriebetrieben |
| **mechanical** [mə'kænɪkl] | mechanisch |
| **pull** [pʊl] | ziehen |
| **chain** [tʃeɪn] | Kette |
| **clever** ['klevə] | geschickt gemacht |
| **might** [maɪt] | könnte(n) (vielleicht) |
| **aeroplane** ['eərəpleɪn] | Flugzeug |
| **wrap** [ræp] | (ein)wickeln |
| **bubble wrap** ['bʌbl ræp] | Luftpolsterfolie |
| **cardboard** ['kɑ:dbɔ:d] | Pappe |
| **perhaps** [pə'hæps] | vielleicht |
| **plane** [pleɪn] | Flugzeug |
| **hand luggage** ['hænd lʌgɪdʒ] | Handgepäck |
| **credit card** ['kredɪt kɑ:d] | Kreditkarte |
| **sign** [saɪn] | unterschreiben |
| **borrow** ['bɒrəʊ] | (sich etw) borgen |
| **pen** [pen] | Stift |
| **trip** [trɪp] | Reise |
| **lend** [lend] | leihen |

59

| | |
|---|---|
| **illustrated** ['ɪləstreɪtɪd] | illustriert |
| **calendar** ['kælɪndə] | Kalender |
| **mountain** ['maʊntən] | (größerer) Berg |
| **cute** [kju:t] | niedlich |
| **look for** ['lʊk fə] | suchen |
| **gift** [gɪft] | Geschenk |
| **sculpture** ['skʌlptʃə] | Plastik, Skulptur |
| **composer** [kəm'pəʊzə] | Komponist/in |
| **heavy** ['hevi] | schwer |
| **imitation** [ˌɪmɪ'teɪʃn] | Imitation |
| **marble** ['mɑ:bl] | Marmor |
| **promise** ['prɒmɪs] | versprechen |
| **carry** ['kæri] | tragen |
| **poison** ['pɔɪzn] | Gift |

60

| | |
|---|---|
| **stamp** [stæmp] | Briefmarke |
| **break** [breɪk] | zerbrechen |
| **cheque card** ['tʃek kɑ:d] | Scheckkarte |
| **gift wrap** ['gɪftræp] | als Geschenk verpacken |

| | |
|---|---|
| **across** [ə'krɒs] | auf die andere/der anderen Seite von |
| **accept** [ək'sept] | annehmen, akzeptieren |
| **biro** ['baɪrəʊ] | Kuli, Kugelschreiber |
| **advice** [əd'vaɪs] | (guter) Rat, Ratschläge |

61

| | |
|---|---|
| **enough** [ɪ'nʌf] | ausreichend, genug |
| **smoke** [sməʊk] | rauchen |
| **purse** [pɜ:s] | Portemonnaie |
| **plenty** ['plenti] | genügend |
| **hurry** ['hʌri] | sich beeilen |

62

| | |
|---|---|
| **recommend** [ˌrekə'mend] | empfehlen |
| **suggest** [sə'dʒest] | vorschlagen |

63

| | |
|---|---|
| **common** ['kɒmən] | gemeinsam |
| **currency** ['kʌrənsi] | Währung |
| **Austria** ['ɒstriə] | Österreich |
| **Belgium** ['beldʒəm] | Belgien |
| **Czech Republic** [tʃek rɪ'pʌblɪk] | Tschechische Republik |
| **Denmark** ['denmɑ:k] | Dänemark |
| **Finland** ['fɪnlənd] | Finnland |
| **Greece** [gri:s] | Griechenland |
| **Hungary** ['hʌŋgəri] | Ungarn |
| **Ireland** ['aɪələnd] | Irland |
| **Luxembourg** ['lʌksəmbɜ:g] | Luxemburg |
| **Netherlands, the ~** ['neðələndz] | (die) Niederlande |
| **Poland** ['pəʊlənd] | Polen |
| **Portugal** ['pɔ:tʃʊgl] | Portugal |
| **Slovakia** [sləʊ'vækiə] | Slowakei |
| **Spain** [speɪn] | Spanien |
| **Sweden** ['swi:dn] | Schweden |
| **Switzerland** ['swɪtsələnd] | (die) Schweiz |
| **UK, the ~** [ju: 'keɪ] | Vereinigtes Königreich |
| **map** [mæp] | Landkarte |
| **capital** ['kæpɪtl] | Hauptstadt |
| **Australia** [ɒ'streɪliə] | Australien |
| **Canada** ['kænədə] | Kanada |
| **China** ['tʃaɪnə] | China |
| **Croatia** [krəʊ'eɪʃə] | Kroatien |
| **Egypt** ['i:dʒɪpt] | Ägypten |
| **Britain** ['brɪtn] | Britannien, Großbritannien |
| **India** ['ɪndiə] | Indien |
| **Israel** ['ɪzreɪl] | Israel |
| **Japan** [dʒə'pæn] | Japan |
| **Mexico** ['meksɪkəʊ] | Mexiko |
| **Russia** ['rʌʃə] | Russland |
| **Turkey** ['tɜ:ki] | Türkei |

## Unit 10

65

| | |
|---|---|
| **department store** [dɪ'pɑ:tmənt stɔ:] | Kaufhaus, Warenhaus |
| **floor** [flɔ:] | Etage, Stockwerk |
| **bag** [bæg] | Tasche |
| **leather** ['leðə] | Leder |
| **china** ['tʃaɪnə] | Porzellan |
| **basement** ['beɪsment] | Untergeschoss |
| **ground floor** [ˌgraʊnd 'flɔ:] | Erdgeschoss |
| **stationery** ['steɪʃənri] | Briefpapier |
| **carpet** ['kɑ:pɪt] | Teppich |
| **electrical** [ɪ'lektrɪkl] | elektrisch |
| **fabric** ['fæbrɪk] | Stoff |
| **furniture** ['fɜ:nɪtʃə] | Möbel |
| **haberdashery** ['hæbədæʃəri] | Kurzwaren |
| **textiles** ['tekstaɪlz] | Textilien |
| **jewellery** ['dʒu:əlri] | Schmuck |
| **ladies' wear** ['leɪdiz weə] | Damenbekleidung |
| **lamp** [læmp] | Lampe |
| **men's wear** ['menz weə] | Herrenbekleidung |
| **camping** ['kæmpɪŋ] | Camping |
| **accessory** [ək'sesəri] | Accessoire |
| **chart** [tʃɑ:t] | Diagramm, Tabelle |

65t

| | |
|---|---|
| **curtains** ['kɜ:tnz] | Vorhänge |
| **towel** ['taʊəl] | Handtuch |
| **tablecloth** ['teɪblklɒθ] | Tischdecke |
| **luggage** ['lʌgɪdʒ] | Gepäck |
| **visit** ['vɪzɪt] | besuchen |
| **pure** [pjʊə] | rein |
| **gentleman** ['dʒentlmən] | Herr |
| **pattern** ['pætn] | Muster |
| **miss** [mɪs] | verpassen |
| **bargain** ['bɑ:gɪn] | Sonderangebot |
| **porcelain** ['pɔ:səlɪn] | Porzellan |
| **dinnerware** ['dɪnəweə] | Geschirr |
| **various** ['veəriəs] | verschiedene(r) |
| **washing machine** ['wɒʃɪŋ məʃi:n] | Waschmaschine |
| **dishwasher** ['dɪʃwɒʃə] | Geschirrspülmaschine |
| **microwave oven** [ˌmaɪkrəweɪv 'ʌvn] | Mikrowellenherd |

66

| | |
|---|---|
| **upstairs** [ˌʌp'steəz] | oben |
| **downstairs** [ˌdaʊn'steəz] | unten |
| **lift** [lɪft] | Fahrstuhl |
| **button** ['bʌtn] | Knopf |
| **zip** [zɪp] | Reißverschluss |
| **doll** [dɒl] | Puppe |
| **pressure cooker** ['preʃə kʊkə] | Schnellkochtopf |
| **mattress** ['mætrəs] | Matratze |
| **wrist watch** ['rɪst wɒtʃ] | Armbanduhr |
| **fountain pen** ['faʊntən pen] | Füller |
| **escalator** ['eskəleɪtə] | Rolltreppe |
| **out of order** [aʊt əv 'ɔ:də] | außer Betrieb |
| **stairs** [steəz] | Treppe |
| **oriental** [ˌɔ:ri'entl] | orientalisch |
| **rug** [rʌg] | Vorleger, Teppich |
| **tent** [tent] | Zelt |

67

| | |
|---|---|
| **try on** [ˌtraɪ 'ɒn] | anprobieren |
| **teddy bear** ['tedibeə] | Teddybär |
| **silk** [sɪlk] | Seide |
| **tie** [taɪ] | Krawatte |
| **suntan lotion** ['sʌntæn ləʊʃn] | Bräunungslotion |
| **bath-towel** ['bɑ:θ taʊəl] | Bade(hand)tuch |
| **walkman** ['wɔ:kmən] | Walkman |
| **jacket** ['dʒækɪt] | Jacke |
| **nightdress** ['naɪtdres] | Nachthemd |
| **prettier** ['prɪtiə] | hübscher |
| **cheaper** ['tʃi:pə] | billiger |
| **get sth mixed up** [get ˌmɪkst 'ʌp] | verwechseln |
| **look like** ['lʊk laɪk] | aussehen |
| **tall** [tɔ:l] | groß |
| **keep on** [ˌki:p 'ɒn] | weitermachen |
| **grow** [grəʊ] | wachsen |

| | |
|---|---|
| **blond** [blɒnd] | blond |
| **curly** [kɜːlɪ] | lockig |
| **photograph** ['fəʊtəʊ, 'fəʊtəgrɑːf] | Foto |

68

| | |
|---|---|
| **comparison** [kəm'pærɪsn] | Vergleich, Steigerung |
| **worse** [wɜːs] | schlechter, schlimmer |
| **worst** [wɜːst] | am schlechtesten, am schlimmsten |
| **least** [liːst] | am wenigsten |
| **comfortable** ['kʌmftəbl] | bequem |

69

| | |
|---|---|
| **spend** [spend] | ausgeben |
| **housing** ['haʊzɪŋ] | Wohnungen |
| **health** [helθ] | Gesundheit |
| **fuel** ['fjuːəl] | Brennstoff |
| **power** ['paʊə] | Energie |
| **percentage** [pə'sentɪdʒ] | Prozentsatz |
| **alcohol** ['ælkəhɒl] | Alkohol |
| **tobacco** [tə'bækəʊ] | Tabak |
| **clothes** [kləʊðz] | Kleidung, Kleider |
| **transport** ['trænspɔːt] | Verkehr(smittel) |
| **communication** [kəˌmjuːnɪ'keɪʃn] | Kommunikation |
| **rent** [rent] | Miete |
| **gas** [gæs] | Gas |
| **electricity** [ɪˌlek'trɪsəti] | Strom |
| **leisure** ['leʒə ] | Freizeit |
| **medical insurance** [ˌmedɪkl ɪn'ʃʊərəns] | Krankenversicherung |
| **located** [ləʊ'keɪtɪd] | sich befinden in |
| **popular** ['pɒpjələ] | beliebt |
| **start out** [ˌstɑːt 'aʊt] | anfangen |
| **merchant** ['mɜːtʃənt] | Händler |
| **tourist attraction** [ˌtʊərɪst ə'trækʃn] | Touristenattraktion |
| **special** ['speʃl] | besondere(r,s) |
| **Christmas** ['krɪsməs] | Weihnachten |
| **opening hours** ['əʊpənɪŋ aʊəz] | Geschäfts-, Öffnungszeiten |

70

| | |
|---|---|
| **directions** [də'rekʃnz] | Wegbeschreibung |
| **outside** [aut'saɪd] | außerhalb (von) |
| **route** [ruːt] | Route, Strecke |
| **cross** [krɒs] | überqueren |
| **far** [fɑː] | weit (entfernt) |
| **railway station** ['reɪlweɪ steɪʃn] | Bahnhof |
| **bus stop** ['bʌs stɒp] | Bushaltestelle |
| **gallery** ['gæləri] | (Kunst)galerie |
| **theatre** ['θɪətə] | Theater |

71

| | |
|---|---|
| **change** [tʃeɪndʒ] | umsteigen |
| **traffic lights** ['træfɪk laɪts] | (Verkehrs-)Ampel |
| **junction** ['dʒʌŋkʃn] | Kreuzung |
| **along** [ə'lɒŋ] | entlang |
| **tourist** ['tʊərɪst] | Tourist/in |
| **interesting** ['ɪntrəstɪŋ] | interessant |
| **public** ['pʌblɪk] | öffentlich |
| **clue** [kluː] | Hinweis |
| **one way** [ˌwʌn 'weɪ] | Einbahn- |
| **museum** [mju'zɪəm] | Museum |

## Unit 11

72

| | |
|---|---|
| **matter** ['mætə] | Sache; etw ausmachen |
| **blouse** [blauz] | Bluse |
| **rack** [ræk] | Stange |
| **match** [mætʃ] | (zusammen) passen |
| **sleeve** [sliːv] | Ärmel |
| **sleeved** [sliːvd] | ärmelig |
| **pale** [peɪl] | hell |
| **pinstriped** ['pɪnstraɪpt] | mit Nadelstreifen |
| **patterned** ['pætənd] | gemustert |
| **label** ['leɪbl] | Etikett |
| **temperature** ['temprətʃə] | Temperatur |
| **damp** [dæmp] | feucht |
| **striped** [straɪpt] | gestreift |
| **synthetic** [sɪn'θetɪk] | synthetisch |
| **fitting room** ['fɪtɪŋ ruːm] | Anprobe(kabine) |

73

| | |
|---|---|
| **suit** [suːt] | stehen, passen |
| **fit** [fɪt] | passen |
| **turquoise** ['tɜːkwɔɪz] | türkis |
| **navy** ['neɪvi] | Marine |
| **purple** ['pɜːpl] | lila |
| **polka dot** ['pɒlkə dɒt] | Punktmuster |
| **tartan** ['tɑːtn] | Schottenkaro |

74

| | |
|---|---|
| **care** [keə] | Pflege |
| **tumble-dry** [ˌtʌmbl 'draɪ] | (im Trommeltrockner) trocknen |
| **tumble-dryer** [ˌtʌmbl 'draɪə] | Trommeltrockner |
| **wool** [wʊl] | Wolle |
| **hand-washed** ['hændwɒʃt] | von Hand gewaschen |
| **setting** ['setɪŋ] | Einstellung |
| **dry-clean** [ˌdrʌɪ 'kliːn] | chemisch reinigen |
| **bleach** [bliːtʃ] | bleichen |
| **jumper** ['dʒʌmpə] | Pullover |

75

| | |
|---|---|
| **stonewashed** ['stəʊnwɒʃt] | stonewashed |
| **button fly** ['bʌtn flaɪ] | Hosenschlitz mit Knöpfen |
| **waist** [weɪst] | Taille |
| **longer** ['lɒŋgə] | länger |
| **zip fly** ['zɪp flaɪ] | Hosenschlitz mit Reißverschluss |
| **tight** [taɪt] | eng |
| **drainpipe** ['dreɪnpaɪp] | Röhrenhosen |
| **loose** [luːs] | weit (geschnitten) |
| **baggy** ['bægi] | ausgebeult, sackartig |
| **boot leg** ['buːtleg] | Bootleg- |
| **measure** ['meʒə] | messen |
| **length** [leŋθ] | Länge |

76

| | |
|---|---|
| **British** ['brɪtɪʃ] | britisch |
| **dress** [dres] | Kleid |
| **response** [rɪ'spɒns] | Antwort |
| **shorten** ['ʃɔːtn] | kürzen |
| **light** [laɪt] | hell |
| **shoulder** ['ʃəʊldə] | Schulter |
| **perfectly** ['pɜːfɪktli] | perfekt |

77

| | |
|---|---|
| **belt** [belt] | Gürtel |
| **boot** [buːt] | Stiefel |
| **briefcase** ['briːfkeɪs] | Aktentasche |
| **cardigan** ['kɑːdɪgən] | Strickjacke |

**high heel** [ˌhaɪ 'hi:l] hoher Absatz
**leggings** ['legɪŋz] Leggings
**polo-neck** ['pəʊləʊnek] Rollkragen
**round-neck** ['raʊnd nek] Rundkragen
**sandal** ['sændl] Sandale
**scarf** [skɑ:f] Schal
**skirt** [skɜ:t] Rock
**sweatshirt** ['swetʃɜ:t] Sweatshirt
**stockings** ['stɒkɪŋz] Strümpfe
**tracksuit bottoms** ['træksu:t 'bɒtəmz] Trainingshose
**vest** [vest] Unterhemd

78

**model** ['mɒdl] Modell
**announcer** [ə'naʊnsə] Sprecher/in

78t

**lovely** ['lʌvli] schön, hübsch
**casual** ['kæʒuel] leger
**outfit** ['aʊtfɪt] Ensemble, Kleidung
**smart** [smɑ:t] schick
**sporty** ['spɔ:ti] sportlich
**trainers** [treɪnə] Turnschuhe
**stylish** [staɪlɪʃ] elegant, modisch

78

**coat** [kəʊt] Mantel, Jacke

79

**button-down collar** [ˌbʌtndaʊn 'kɒlə] geknöpfter Kragen
**clothing** ['kləʊðɪŋ] Kleidung, Kleider
**ending** ['endɪŋ] Ende (der Geschichte)

## Unit 12

80

**solve** [sɒlv] lösen
**sole** [səʊl] Sohle
**since** [sɪns] seit
**branch** [brɑ:ntʃ] Filiale
**under guarantee** [ˌʌndə ˌgærən'ti:] mit Garantie

81

**CD player** [ˌsi: 'di: pleɪə] CD-Player, CD-Spieler
**manufacturer** [ˌmænju'fæktʃərə] Hersteller/in
**lose** [lu:z] verlieren
**case** [keɪs] Fall
**expire** [ɪk'spaɪə] ablaufen
**anyway** ['eniweɪ] jedenfalls
**estimate** ['estɪmət] (Kosten-)Voranschlag
**whether** ['weðə] ob
**complain** [kəm'pleɪn] sich beklagen

82

**consumer rights** [kən'sju:mə raɪts] Verbraucherrechte
**once** [wʌns] wenn einmal
**yet** [jet] noch
**turn out to be** [ˌtɜ:n 'aʊt tə bi] sich herausstellen
**faulty** ['fɔ:lti] fehlerhaft
**refund** ['ri:fʌnd] Rückzahlung, Erstattung
**deal with** ['di:l wɪð] sich befassen mit
**complaint** [kəm'pleɪnt] Beschwerde, Klage
**wear** [weə] tragen, anhaben
**return** [rɪ'tɜ:n] zurückgeben

84

**TV-set** [ˌti:'vi: set] Fernsehgerät
**apologize** [ə'pɒlədʒaɪz] sich entschuldigen
**delay** [dɪ'leɪ] Verspätung
**awfully** ['ɔ:fli] schrecklich
**offer** ['ɒfə] anbieten
**discount** ['dɪskaʊnt] Rabatt
**credit note** ['kredɪt nəʊt] (Rechnungs-)Gutschrift
**amount** [ə'maʊnt] Summe, Betrag

85

**mouldy** ['məʊldi] verschimmelt
**peculiar** [ˌpɪ'kju:liə] eigen(artig)
**off** [ɒf] schlecht
**scratch** [skrætʃ] kratzen
**shrink** [ʃrɪŋk] schrumpfen, eingehen
**even though** ['i:vn ðəʊ] obwohl
**shrink resistant** [ˌʃrɪŋk rɪ'zɪstənt] nicht einlaufend
**spin dry** [ˌspɪn 'draɪ] trockenschleudern
**sofa** ['səʊfə] Sofa
**receive** [rɪ'si:v] bekommen
**drop** [drɒp] fallen (lassen)
**film** [fɪlm] Film
**cork** [kɔ:k] Korken
**suitable** ['su:təbl] passend
**come off** [kʌm ɒf] sich ablösen
**be able to** [bi 'eɪbl tə] können

86

**occur** [ə'kɜ:] geschehen

87

**born** [bɔ:n] geboren
**apology** [ə'pɒlədʒi] Entschuldigung(sschreiben)
**dependence** [dɪ'pendəns] Abhängigkeit
**expiry** [ɪk'spaɪəri] Verfall(sdatum)
**reduction** [rɪ'dʌkʃn] Preisnachlass
**suggestion** [sə'dʒestʃən] Vorschlag
**solution** [sə'lu:ʃn] Lösung

87p

**part** [pɑ:t] Rolle
**remember** [rɪ'membə] sich erinnern
**degrees** [dɪ'gri:z] Grad
**hair-dryer** ['heədraɪə] Fön
**air** [eə] Luft
**rotten** ['rɒtn] verdorben
**low** [ləʊ] niedrig
**expect** [ɪk'spekt] erwarten
**appliance** [ə'plaɪəns] Gerät
**repairs** [rɪ'peəz] Reparaturen

88

**business correspondence** [ˌbɪznəs ˌkɒrɪ'spɒndəns] Geschäftsbriefe, Handelskorrespondenz
**layout** ['leɪaʊt] Layout
**abbreviation** [əˌbri:vi'eɪʃn] Abkürzung
**limited company** [ˌlɪmɪtɪd 'kʌmpəni] Gesellschaft mit beschränkter Haftung (GmbH)
**reference (ref)** ['refərəns] Zeichen, Bezug

89

**supply** [sə'plaɪ] liefern; Lieferung
**dated** ['deɪtɪd] datiert
**grateful** ['greɪtfl] dankbar
**willing to** ['wɪlɪŋ tə] gewillt (sein), bereitwillig

| | |
|---|---|
| **trade discount** ['treɪd dɪskaʊnt] | Händlerrabatt |
| **list price** ['lɪst praɪs] | Listenpreis |
| **further** ['fɜːðə] | weitere(s, r) |
| **cash discount** ['kæʃ dɪskaʊnt] | Skonto, Rabatt bei Sofortzahlung |
| **payment** ['peɪmənt] | Bezahlung |
| **yours sincerely** [jɔːz sɪn'sɪəli] | Mit freundlichen Grüßen |
| **firm** [fɜːm] | Firma |
| **letterhead** ['letəhed] | Briefkopf |
| **salutation** [ˌsælju'teɪʃn] | Anrede |
| **subject** ['sʌbdʒɪkt] | Thema |
| **complimentary close** [ˌkɒmplɪˌmentri 'kləʊz] | Schlussformel |
| **signature block** ['sɪgnətʃə blɒk] | Unterschriftsabschnitt |

90

| | |
|---|---|
| **envelope** ['envələʊp] | (Brief-)Umschlag |
| **postcode** ['pəʊstkəʊd] | Postleitzahl |
| **county** ['kaʊnti] | Grafschaft |
| **ZIP code** ['zɪp kəʊd] | Postleitzahl |
| **initials** [ɪ'nɪʃlz] | Initialen |
| **Asian** ['eɪʃn] | asiatisch |
| **yours faithfully** [jɔːz 'feɪθfəli] | Mit freundlichen Grüßen |
| **truly** ['truːli] | wahrhaftig |
| **unmarried** [ˌʌn'mærid] | unverheiratet |
| **either** ['aɪðə] | entweder |
| **signature** ['sɪgnətʃə] | Unterschrift |
| **sender** ['sendə] | Absender |

91

| | |
|---|---|
| **consignment** [kən'saɪnmənt] | Lieferung, Versendung |
| **incorrect** [ˌɪnkə'rekt] | fehlerhaft |
| **instead** [ɪn'sted] | anstatt |

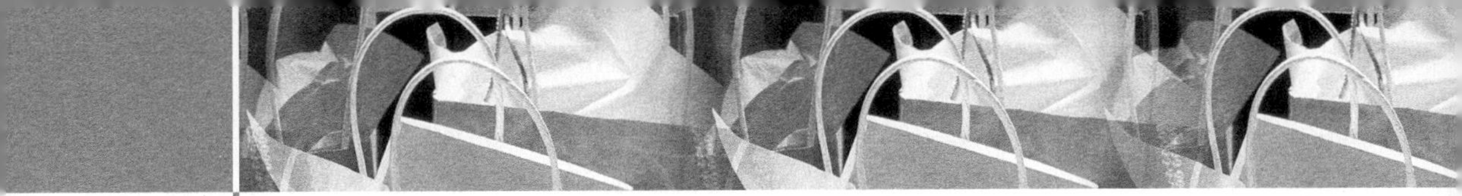

# *A–Z word list*

Diese Liste enthält alle Wörter in alphabetischer Reihenfolge. Es sind jedoch die Wörter, die zum Grundwortschatz gehören, hier nicht aufgeführt. (Siehe Basic Word list.)

p = das Wort befindet sich im *pairwork file.*
t = das Wort befindet sich im *transcript.*

## A

**a bit** *6* recht, ziemlich
**a long way** *30p* ein weiter Weg
**abbreviation** *88* Abkürzung
**abroad** *57* im Ausland
**accept** *60* annehmen, akzeptieren
**accessory** *65* Accessoire
**across** *60* auf die andere/der anderen Seite von
**act out** *43* durchspielen
**actually** *55* eigentlich
**add** *22* hinzufügen
**advertisement (ad)** *24* Anzeige
**advice** *60* (guter) Rat, Ratschläge
**aeroplane** *58* Flugzeug
**afraid, I'm ~** *20* leider
**ago** *51* vor
**agree** *32* übereinstimmen
**air** *87p* Luft
**airport** *56* Flughafen
**aisle** *19* Gang
**alarm clock** *26* Wecker
**alcohol** *69* Alkohol
**all right** *52* in Ordnung, (schon) gut
**along** *71* entlang
**altogether** *15t* insgesamt, im Ganzen
**am** *24* vor 12 Uhr
**American** *13* Amerikaner/in; amerikanisch
**amount** *84* Summe, Betrag
**announcer** *78* Sprecher/in
**any more** *56p* nicht ... mehr
**anything else** *12* sonst noch etwas
**anyway** *81* jedenfalls
**apologize** *84* sich entschuldigen
**apology** *87* Entschuldigung(sschreiben)
**apple strudel** *40* Apfelstrudel
**appliance** *87p* Gerät
**apricot** *40* Aprikose
**aquarium** *30p* Aquarium
**article** *26t* Artikel, Gegenstand
**Asian** *90* asiatisch
**assistance** *57* Hilfe
**assistant** *9* Assistent/in
**attention** *50* Aufmerksamkeit
**Australia** *63* Australien
**Austria** *63* Österreich
**Austrian** *9* österreichisch
**available** *54* erhältlich
**avocado** *46* Avocado
**awfully** *84* schrecklich

## B

**back garden** *11* Garten (hinter dem Haus)
**background** *56p* Hintergrund
**bacon** *22* Schinkenspeck
**badly** *33* sehr, schlecht
**bag** *65* Tasche
**baggy** *75* ausgebeult, sackartig
**bake** *46* backen
**bakery** *37* Bäckerei
**band** *24* (Musik-)Kapelle
**bar of chocolate** *38* Tafel Schokolade
**barbecue sauce** *46* Grillsauce
**bargain** *65t* Sonderangebot
**basement** *65* Untergeschoss
**bath-towel** *67* Bade(hand)tuch
**batter** *44* Eierteig
**battery** *58* Batterie
**battery operated** *58* batteriebetrieben
**be able to** *85* können
**be away** *54t* weg sein
**be interested in sth** *11* sich interessieren für
**beans** *22* Bohnen
**bedlinen** *52* Bettwäsche
**beef** *46* Rindfleisch
**behind** *19* hinter, hinten
**Belgium** *63* Belgien
**believe** *32* glauben
**belong to** *20* (dazu) gehören, angehören
**below** *8* unten(stehend)
**belt** *77* Gürtel
**best before date** *23* Verfallsdatum
**best selling** *57* absatzstark
**best wishes** *24* Viele Grüße, Alles Gute
**between** *19* zwischen
**beverage** *46* Getränk
**bill** *15t* Rechnung
**biro** *60* Kuli, Kugelschreiber
**biscuit** *18* Keks
**blackberry** *44* Brombeere
**bleach** *74* bleichen
**blond** *67* blond
**blouse** *72* Bluse
**boil** *49* kochen
**boot** *77* Stiefel
**boot leg** *75* Bootleg-
**born** *87* geboren
**borrow** *58* (sich etw) borgen
**both** *17* beide
**bottle** *12* Flasche
**bowl** *50* Schüssel
**box** *6* Kiste, Karton
**branch** *80* Filiale
**brand** *57* Marke
**break** *60* zerbrechen
**breast** *46* Brust
**briefcase** *77* Aktentasche
**bright** *54* leuchtend, hell
**Britain** *63* Britannien, Großbritannien
**British** *76* britisch
**Briton** *13* Brite/Britin
**bubble wrap** *58* Luftpolsterfolie
**building** *15t* Gebäude
**bunch** *15* Bund
**bus stop** *70* Bushaltestelle
**business correspondence** *88* Geschäftsbriefe, Handelskorrespondenz
**busy** *6* beschäftigt
**butcher** *37* Fleischer/in
**buttered** *46* mit Butter bestrichen
**button** *66* Knopf
**button fly** *75* Hosenschlitz mit Knöpfen
**button-down collar** *79* geknöpfter Kragen

## C

**cabbage** *49* Kohl
**calculator** *33* Taschenrechner
**calendar** *59* Kalender
**camping** *65* Camping
**Canada** *63* Kanada
**canteen** *11* Kantine
**capital** *63* Hauptstadt
**cardboard** *58* Pappe
**cardigan** *77* Strickjacke
**cardinal number** *15* Kardinalzahl
**care** *74* Pflege
**care for** *47* gerne haben
**careful** *23* vorsichtig
**carefully** *33* sorgfältig
**carpenter** *11* Zimmermann, Tischler/in

**carpet** *65* Teppich
**carrier bag** *40* Tragetüte
**carrot** *14* Karotte, Möhre
**carry** *59* tragen
**case** *81* Fall
**cash** *35* Bargeld
**cash discount** *89* Skonto, Rabatt bei Sofortzahlung
**cashier** *6* Kassierer/in
**casual** *78t* leger
**cat food** *19* Katzenfutter
**catalogue** *52* Katalog
**catch** *26* erreichen, nehmen
**cauliflower** *22* Blumenkohl
**CD player** *81* CD-Player, CD-Spieler
**central heating system** *11* Zentralheizungsanlage
**certain** *28* sicher, gewiss, bestimmt
**certainly** *12* sicher, gerne
**chain** *58* Kette
**change** *16* Wechselgeld, Kleingeld; *71* umsteigen
**chart** *65* Diagramm, Tabelle
**cheap** *57* billig
**cheaper** *67* billiger
**check** *28* kontrollieren, (über)prüfen
**checkout** *6* Kasse
**cheers** *45* Prost!
**cheese and biscuits** *46* Käse und Kekse
**cheesecake** *44* Käsekuchen
**chemist** *37* Apotheke
**cheque card** *60* Scheckkarte
**chicken** *22* Huhn, Hähnchen
**chicken wings** *46* Hähnchenflügel
**chilli** *46* Chili
**China** *63* China
**china** *65* Porzellan
**Chinese** *49* chinesisch
**chips** *44* Pommes frites
**choice** *46* Wahl, Auswahl
**choose** *19* wählen, aussuchen
**chop** *49* Kotelett
**Christmas** *69* Weihnachten
**cinnamon** *40* Zimt
**clean** *21* reinigen
**cleaning products** *22* Putzmittel
**clever** *58* geschickt gemacht
**clock-face** *58* Zifferblatt
**clothes** *69* Kleidung, Kleider
**clothing** *79* Kleidung, Kleider
**clue** *71* Hinweis
**coat** *78* Mantel, Jacke
**cod** *46* Kabeljau
**coin** *14* Münze
**cola** *44* Cola
**colleague** *6* Kollege, Kollegin
**collection** *56p* Kollektion
**come off** *85* sich ablösen
**come on** *6* beeil dich, los
**comfortable** *68* bequem
**common** *63* gemeinsam
**communication** *69* Kommunikation
**compare** *31* vergleichen
**comparison** *68* Vergleich, Steigerung
**complain** *81* sich beklagen
**complaint** *82* Beschwerde, Klage
**complete** *10* vervollständigen, ergänzen
**completely** *33* völlig
**complimentary close** *89* Schlussformel
**composer** *59* Komponist/in
**computer game** *24* Computerspiel
**consignment** *91* Lieferung, Versendung
**consumer rights** *82* Verbraucher-rechte
**contact lens cleaner** *38* Kontaktlinsenreiniger
**contain** *40* enthalten
**continue** *47* (sich) fortsetzen, fortfahren
**contrasting** *56p* kontrastrierend
**conversation** *47* Gespräch
**cooker** *49* Herd
**copy** *8* abschreiben, kopieren
**coq au vin** *46* Hähnchen in Weinsoße
**cork** *85* Korken
**corner** *19* Ecke
**correct** *8* richtig, korrekt
**cosmetics** *22* Kosmetik(a)
**cost** *14* Kosten; kosten
**cotton** *56p* Baumwolle
**county** *90* Grafschaft
**couple** *39* ein paar, einige
**cracked** *23* angestoßen
**creamy** *46* sahnig
**credit card** *58* Kreditkarte
**credit note** *84* (Rechnungs-) Gutschrift
**crispy** *46* knusprig
**Croatia** *63* Kroatien
**cross** *70* überqueren
**crumble** *44* mit Streusel
**crumbly** *44* krümelig
**cube** *50* Würfel
**cuckoo (clock)** *58* Kuckuck(suhr)
**cuisine** *49* Küche
**curly** *67* lockig
**currency** *63* Währung
**curtains** *65t* Vorhänge
**cushion** *54* Kissen
**custard** *46* Vanillesoße
**customer** *8t* Kunde, Kundin
**cut** *50* (zer-/durch)schneiden
**cute** *59* niedlich
**cycling** *24* Radfahren
**Czech Republic** *63* Tschechische Republik

## D

**daily** *27* täglich, Tages-
**dairy products** *18* Milchprodukte
**damaged** *33* beschädigt
**damp** *72* feucht
**dated** *89* datiert
**daughter-in-law** *10* Schwieger-tochter
**deal with** *82* sich befassen mit
**decide** *55* (sich) entscheiden
**decision** *31* Entscheidung
**decorate** *8t* schmücken, dekorieren
**deep fry** *49* in Fett backen
**degrees** *87p* Grad
**delay** *84* Verspätung
**deli counter** *8t* Feinkoststand
**delicious** *40* köstlich, lecker
**deliver** *23* liefern
**delivery** *54* Lieferung
**Denmark** *63* Dänemark
**department** *52* Abteilung
**department store** *65* Kaufhaus, Warenhaus
**depend on** *57* abhängen von
**dependence** *87* Abhängigkeit
**describe** *8* beschreiben
**desert** *49* Wüste
**design** *56p* Muster
**dessert** *44* Nachspeise, Dessert
**detergents** *22* Reinigungsmittel, Waschmittel
**dial** *56* wählen
**diary** *56* Terminkalender
**dictionary** *22* Wörterbuch
**different** *31* verschieden
**difficult** *47* schwer, schwierig
**dinner party** *50* Abendgesellschaft
**dinnerware** *65t* Geschirr
**dip** *46* Dip
**direct** *56* direkt
**directions** *70* Wegbeschreibung
**directly** *33* direkt
**dirty** *23* schmutzig
**disagree** *32* nicht übereinstimmen
**discount** *84* Rabatt
**dish** *44* Gericht
**dishwasher** *65t* Geschirrspül-maschine
**distance** *15t* Entfernung, Abstand
**divorced** *24* geschieden
**doll** *66* Puppe
**done** *50* gar
**double** *46* Doppel-
**doughnut** *14* Krapfen, Pfannkuchen
**downstairs** *66* unten
**dozen** *38* Dutzend
**drainpipe** *75* Röhrenhosen
**draw** *11* zeichnen
**dress** *6* dekorieren; *76* Kleid
**drink** *22* Getränk
**drive** *35* (Auto)fahren
**drop** *85* fallen (lassen)
**dry-clean** *74* chemisch reinigen
**duck** *46* Ente
**dumpling** *49* Knödel
**during** *26t* während
**duvet cover** *52* Tagesdecke

## E

**earn** *15t* verdienen
**Egypt** *63* Ägypten
**either** *90* entweder
**electrical** *65* elektrisch
**electricity** *69* Strom
**elephant** *57* Elefant

**empty** *33* leer
**ending** *79* Ende (der Geschichte)
**engaged** *52* besetzt
**enjoy** *32* genießen, gern haben/tun
**enough** *61* ausreichend, genug
**enter** *34* hineingehen, betreten
**entrance** *18* Eingang
**envelope** *90* (Brief-)Umschlag
**environmentally friendly** *31* umweltfreundlich
**escalator** *66* Rolltreppe
**estimate** *81* (Kosten-)Voranschlag
**etc** *17* usw.
**even if** *31* selbst wenn
**even though** *85* obwohl
**exact** *33* genau
**exactly** *15t* genau
**example** *8* Beispiel
**excerpt** *56* Auszug
**exchange** *24* austauschen
**exercise** *8* Übung
**exit** *18* Ausgang
**expect** *87p* erwarten
**expensive** *57* teuer
**expire** *81* ablaufen
**expiry** *87* Verfall(sdatum)
**explain** *49* erklären
**express** *39* ausdrücken
**expression** *40* Ausdruck
**extension** *52* Apparat, Durchwahl

## F

**fabric** *65* Stoff
**false** *25* falsch
**family tree** *10* Stammbaum
**famous** *49* berühmt
**far** *70* weit (entfernt)
**fashion boutique** *37* Modeboutique
**faulty** *82* fehlerhaft
**favourite** *24* Lieblings-
**feature** *57* Merkmal
**feed** *56* füttern
**few** *39* ein paar, wenige
**fifties** *24* Fünfziger
**file** *17* Akte
**fill in** *8* ausfüllen
**fill** *36* füllen
**filled with** *40* gefüllt mit
**fillet** *44* Filet
**film** *85* Film
**finally** *38* schließlich, zum Schluss
**find out** *10* herausfinden
**fine** *55* schön
**finely** *50* dünn
**Finland** *63* Finnland
**firm** *89* Firma
**fit** *73* passen
**fitness centre** *26t* Fitnesscenter
**fitted sheet** *56p* Spannbettuch
**fitting room** *72* Anprobe(kabine)
**fix** *21* reparieren
**fizzy** *22* sprudelnd
**flat sheet** *56p* Bettuch
**flat** *35* Wohnung
**floor** *65* Etage, Stockwerk
**florist** *37* Blumenhändler/in
**flour** *18* Mehl
**flower** *11* Blume
**flowered** *56p* geblümt
**follow** *7* folgen
**foreign** *44* Auslands-, ausländisch
**forest fruits** *46* Waldfrüchte
**form** *8* Form; formen
**fountain pen** *66* Füller
**fragile** *57* zerbrechlich
**France** *35* Frankreich
**free range** *31* Freiland-
**freezer** *43* Gefrierschrank, Tiefkühltruhe
**French** *7* französisch; Französisch
**fresh** *23* frisch
**fridge** *23* Kühlschrank
**frozen food** *18* Tiefkühlkost
**frozen** *23t* (tief)gefroren
**fry** *44* braten, frittieren
**fuel** *69* Brennstoff
**full** *8* voll, vollständig
**furniture** *65* Möbel
**further** *89* weitere(s, r)

## G

**gallery** *70* (Kunst)galerie
**gap** *36* Lücke
**garage** *21* (Auto-)Werkstatt
**gardener** *11* Gärtner/in
**garlic bread** *46* Knoblauchbrot
**garlic** *44* Knoblauch
**garnish** *46* garnieren
**gas** *69* Gas
**gentleman** *65t* Herr
**get in touch** *56* (sich) in Verbindung setzen
**get sth mixed up** *67* verwechseln
**get up** *14* aufstehen
**gift wrap** *60* als Geschenk verpacken
**gift** *59* Geschenk
**glue** *38* Klebstoff
**go out** *28* ausgehen
**golden** *46* golden
**good-looking** *9* gut aussehend
**goods** *31* Ware(n)
**grandchildren** *10* Enkel
**granddaughter** *10* Enkelin
**grandson** *10* Enkel
**grape** *37t* Weintraube
**grateful** *89* dankbar
**gravy** *46* Soße
**Greece** *63* Griechenland
**greet** *36t* (be)grüßen
**grill** *46* grillen
**grocer** *37* Lebensmittelhändler/in
**grocery shop** *12* Lebensmittelgeschäft
**ground floor** *65* Erdgeschoss
**grow** *67* wachsen
**guitar** *24* Gitarre
**guy** *6* Kerl, Typ

## H

**haberdashery** *65* Kurzwaren
**habit** *31* Gewohnheit
**hairdresser** *11* Friseur, Friseuse
**hair-dryer** *87p* Fön
**hand** *58* Zeiger, Hand
**hand luggage** *58* Handgepäck
**handle** *23* anfassen, berühren
**hand-washed** *74* von Hand gewaschen
**happen** *35* passieren
**hardly ever** *29* fast nie
**hardly** *32* kaum
**hardware** *37* Eisenwaren, Haushaltswaren
**hate** *28* hassen, gar nicht mögen
**head of lettuce** *38* Salatkopf
**health** *69* Gesundheit
**healthy** *31* gesund
**hear** *15* hören
**heart shaped** *54* herzförmig
**heavy** *59* schwer
**hectic** *31* hektisch
**herb** *46* (Würz)Kraut
**herbs** *22* Kräuter
**here you are** *12* bitte
**high heel** *77* hoher Absatz
**hold on** *54* bleiben Sie dran
**honey** *18* Honig
**hospital** *11* Krankenhaus
**hours** *24* Arbeitszeit
**household budget** *31* Haushaltskasse
**household cleaning products** *18* Haushaltsreiniger
**household electronics** *37* Haushaltselektronik
**housewife** *11* Hausfrau
**housing** *69* Wohnungen
**how do you do** *7* Es ist angenehm, Sie kennen zu lernen.
**Hungarian** *24* Ungarisch
**Hungary** *63* Ungarn
**hurry** *61* sich beeilen
**husband** *10* (Ehe-)Mann

## I

**ideal** *31* ideal
**idealist** *31* Idealist
**identify** *31* erkennen
**illustrated** *59* illustriert
**imitation** *59* Imitation
**important** *23* wichtig
**impulse** *31* Impuls
**in front of** *19* vor
**include** *46* inklusive
**incorrect** *91* fehlerhaft
**India** *63* Indien
**Indian** *49* indisch
**ingredient** *49* Zutat
**initials** *90* Initialen
**inside** *58* innen
**install** *11* installieren, einbauen
**instead** *91* anstatt
**instruction** *50* Anweisung
**insurance company** *11* Versicherungsgesellschaft
**interesting** *71* interessant
**introduce** *6* (sich) vorstellen

**introduction** *7* Vorstellung
**Ireland** *63* Irland
**iron** *38* Bügeleisen
**Israel** *63* Israel
**Italian** *24* Italienisch
**Italy** *41* Italien
**item** *17* Artikel, Gegenstand, Ding

**J**

**jacket** *67* Jacke
**jam** *18* Marmelade, Konfitüre
**Japan** *63* Japan
**jar** *34* Glas
**jeweller** *37* Juwelier/in
**jewellery** *65* Schmuck
**juice** *14* Saft
**juicy** *23t* saftig
**jumper** *74* Pullover
**junction** *71* Kreuzung
**just** *10* einfach, nur, bloß, gerade

**K**

**keep on** *67* weitermachen
**keep s.o. waiting** *56* jdn warten lassen
**kind** *24* Art
**knife** *50* Messer

**L**

**label** *72* Etikett
**ladies' wear** *65* Damenbekleidung
**lamp** *65* Lampe
**lately** *32* in letzter Zeit
**later** *6* später
**layer** *46* Schicht
**layout** *88* Layout
**lead crystal** *57* Bleikristall
**least** *68* am wenigsten
**leather** *65* Leder
**leek** *49* Porree
**left** *54* übrig
**leggings** *77* Leggings
**leisure** *69* Freizeit
**lend** *58* leihen
**length** *75* Länge
**letterhead** *89* Briefkopf
**lift** *66* Fahrstuhl
**light** *44* leicht *76* hell
**lightly** *23* leicht
**liking** *46* Geschmack
**limited company** *88* Gesellschaft mit beschränkter Haftung (GmbH)
**linen** *52* Leinen
**linseed** *40* Leinsamen
**list price** *89* Listenpreis
**listen** *8* zuhören
**litre** *12* Liter
**liver** *49* Leber
**loaf** *38* Laib
**lobster** *22* Hummer
**located** *69* sich befinden in
**longer** *75* länger
**look for** *59* suchen
**look forward to** *24* sich freuen auf
**look like** *67* aussehen
**loose** *75* weit (geschnitten)
**lose** *81* verlieren
**lovely** *78t* schön, hübsch
**low** *87p* niedrig
**Ltd** *52* GmbH
**luggage** *65t* Gepäck
**lunch break** *26* Mittagspause
**lunch** *27* Mittagessen
**Luxembourg** *63* Luxemburg

**M**

**machine** *21* Maschine, Gerät
**mail-order** *52* Postversand
**main course** *44* Hauptgericht
**mainly** *40* hauptsächlich, vor allem
**make up** *19* erfinden, sich ausdenken
**manage** *16* (es) schaffen
**manager** *6* Filialleiter/in, Chef/in
**manufacturer** *81* Hersteller/in
**map** *63* Landkarte
**marble** *59* Marmor
**margarine** *38* Margarine
**mark** *23* Zeichen
**married** *10* verheiratet
**mash** *46* Kartoffelpüree
**mashed** *46* püriert
**match** *14* zuordnen; *72* (zusammen) passen
**material** *54* Stoff
**matter** *72* Sache; etw ausmachen
**mattress** *66* Matratze
**maybe** *44* vielleicht
**meal** *31* Essen
**mean** *23* bedeuten
**measure** *75* messen
**meat** *18* Fleisch
**mechanic** *11* Mechaniker/in
**mechanical** *58* mechanisch
**medical insurance** *69* Krankenversicherung
**melon** *41* Melone
**member** *11* Mitglied
**men's wear** *65* Herrenbekleidung
**menu** *44* Speisekarte, Menü
**merchant** *69* Händler
**message** *51* Nachricht
**Mexico** *63* Mexiko
**microwave oven** *65t* Mikrowellenherd
**might** *58* könnte(n) (vielleicht)
**mind** *56* etw dagegen haben
**miss** *65t* verpassen
**mistake** *23* Fehler
**mix** *50* mischen
**mixture** *44* Mischung
**mobile phone** *51* Handy
**model** *78* Modell
**monitor** *34* Monitor
**mother-in-law** *10* Schwiegermutter
**motorbike** *24* Motorrad
**mouldy** *85* verschimmelt
**mountain** *59* (größerer) Berg
**mousse** *46* Creme
**muffin** *15* Muffin
**museum** *71* Museum
**mushroom** *44* Pilz, Champignon
**musical** *56* Musical
**mustard** *18* Senf

**N**

**navy** *73* Marine
**negative** *7* Verneinung; negativ
**nephew** *10* Neffe
**Netherlands, the ~** *63* Niederlande
**new potato** *41* Frühkartoffel
**news agent** *37* Zeitungshändler
**niece** *10* Nichte
**nightdress** *67* Nachthemd
**note** *16* Note, Schein
**notes** *26* Notizen
**nurse** *11* Krankenpfleger/in
**nut** *23* Nuss
**nutmeg** *22* Muskat

**O**

**occur** *86* geschehen
**of course** *6* natürlich, selbstverständlich
**off** *24* frei *85* schlecht
**off, 30% ~** *56p* Nachlass (von 30%)
**offer** *84* anbieten
**office clerk** *11* Büroangestellte/r
**office** *23* Amt, Büro
**olive** *40* Olive
**once** *6* einmal, wenn einmal
**once** *82* wenn einmal
**one way** *71* Einbahn-
**onion ring** *46* Zwiebelring
**onion** *46* Zwiebel
**onto** *11* auf
**opening hours** *69* Geschäfts-, Öffnungszeiten
**opinion** *32* Meinung
**opposite** *19* gegenüber(liegend)
**optician** *37* Optiker/in
**ordinal number** *21* Ordnungszahl
**ordinary** *57* gewöhnlich
**organic** *31* organisch
**organically grown** *31* biologisch angebaut
**oriental** *66* orientalisch
**out of order** *66* außer Betrieb
**out of sth** *54t* kein mehr haben
**outfit** *78t* Ensemble, Kleidung
**outside** *70* außerhalb (von)
**owl** *57* Eule
**own** *11* eigene/r/s

**P**

**package** *31* Paket, Verpackung
**packaging** *31* Verpackung
**packet** *23* Päckchen, Paket
**painkiller** *38* schmerzstillendes Mittel
**pair** *16* Paar
**pale** *72* hell
**pan** *44* Pfanne
**parsley** *22* Petersilie
**part** *87p* Rolle
**partner** *7* Partner/in
**past** *25* nach
**pasta** *18* Nudeln

**pastel** *56p* pastellfarben
**pastry** *40* Gebäck
**paté** *46* Pastete
**pattern** *65t* Muster
**patterned** *72* gemustert
**pause** *52* Pause
**payment** *89* Bezahlung
**pea** *23t* Erbse
**peanut** *39* Erdnuss
**peculiar** *85* eigen(artig)
**pen** *58* Stift
**pen-friend** *24* Brieffreund/in
**pepper** *46* Paprika(schote)
**percentage** *69* Prozentsatz
**perfectly** *76* perfekt
**perhaps** *58* vielleicht
**personal hygiene articles** *22* Toilettenartikel
**pet food** *18* Tierfutter
**pet** *24* Haustier
**photograph** *67* Foto
**phrase** *29* Redewendung
**pick up** *37t* abholen
**piece** *11* Stück, Blatt
**pill** *37t* Pille
**pillowcase** *52* Kopfkissenbezug
**pineapple** *22* Ananas
**pinstriped** *72* mit Nadelstreifen
**plaice** *49* Scholle
**plain** *56p* einfarbig
**plan** *31* planen
**plane** *58* Flugzeug
**plant** *11* Pflanze
**pleased to meet you** *7* Es freut mich, Sie kennen zu lernen.
**plenty** *61* genügend
**plumber** *11* Klempner/in
**pm** *24* nach 12 Uhr
**poison** *59* Gift
**Poland** *63* Polen
**polite** *16* höflich
**polka dot** *73* Punktmuster
**polo-neck** *77* Rollkragen
**polyester** *56p* Polyester
**poor** *40* schlecht, mangelhaft
**poppy seed** *40* Mohn(samen)
**popular** *69* beliebt
**porcelain** *65t* Porzellan
**pork** *38* Schweinefleisch
**portion** *46* Portion
**Portugal** *63* Portugal
**possible** *30* möglich
**postcode** *90* Postleitzahl
**pot plant** *42* Topfpflanze
**pot** *46* Kanne
**poultry** *18* Geflügel
**pour** *50* gießen
**power** *69* Energie
**practice** *8* Übung, Training
**prawn** *46* Garnele, Krabbe
**prefer** *40* lieber mögen
**pregnant** *23* schwanger
**pressure cooker** *66* Schnellkochtopf
**prettier** *67* hübscher
**pretty** *57* hübsch
**pretzel** *12* Brezel
**print** *56p* Muster
**probably** *32* wahrscheinlich
**product line** *33* Produktlinie
**product** *31* Produkt
**profile** *56* Profil, Beschreibung
**promise** *59* versprechen
**properly** *33* richtig, korrekt
**pub** *55* Kneipe
**public** *71* öffentlich
**pull** *58* ziehen
**pumpkin seed** *40* Kürbiskerne
**pure** *65t* rein
**purple** *73* lila
**purse** *61* Portemonnaie
**put s.o. through** *52* jdn verbinden
**puzzle** *11* Rätsel

## Q

**quarter** *25* Viertel
**question** *7* Frage
**queue** *21t* Schlange
**quick** *33* schnell
**quickly** *31* schnell, rasch
**quiet** *54* ruhig, leise
**quite** *30p* ziemlich, ganz

## R

**rack** *72* Stange
**racket** *42* Schläger
**railway station** *70* Bahnhof
**rain** *14* Regen
**rare** *47* halb roh
**rather** *26t* ziemlich
**raw** *23* roh
**reach** *51* erreichen
**receipt** *16* Quittung, Beleg
**receive** *85* bekommen
**recipe** *50* (Koch-)Rezept
**recommend** *62* empfehlen
**redcurrant jelly** *46* rotes Johannisbeergelee
**reduced** *31* reduziert
**reduction** *87* Preisnachlass
**reference (ref)** *88* Zeichen, Bezug
**refund** *82* Rückzahlung, Erstattung
**related** *47* verwandt
**remember** *87p* sich erinnern
**rent** *69* Miete
**repair** *11* reparieren
**repairs** *87p* Reparaturen
**repeat** *52* wiederholen
**reply** *30p* antworten
**response** *76* Antwort
**rest** *26t* Rest
**retired** *11* im Ruhestand
**return** *82* zurückgeben
**rewrite** *8* umschreiben
**rich** *46* schwer
**ring s.o. back** *51* jdn zurückrufen
**ring** *26* klingeln, läuten
**roast** *46* Braten; braten
**role play** *17* Rollenspiel
**roll** *50* Brötchen
**roof** *50* Dach
**rotten** *87p* verdorben
**round-neck** *77* Rundkragen
**route** *70* Route, Strecke
**routine** *27* Routine
**rucksack** *36t* Rucksack
**rug** *66* Vorleger, Teppich
**run** *8* leiten, führen
**Russia** *63* Russland
**rye** *40* Roggen

## S

**safe** *50* Safe, Tresor
**sailing** *24* Segeln
**sale** *52* Verkauf
**sales** *43* Verkaufs-
**salutation** *89* Anrede
**sandal** *77* Sandale
**sandwich** *15* Sandwich
**sardine** *22* Sardine
**sausage** *18* Wurst
**sauté** *44* (kurz) anbraten
**save** *21* sparen
**scarf** *77* Schal
**science fiction** *30p* Sciencefiction
**scratch** *85* kratzen
**sculpture** *59* Plastik, Skulptur
**seafood** *22* Meeresfrüchte
**season** *30p* Jahreszeit
**seem** *32* (er)scheinen
**selection** *46* Auswahl
**send** *52* schicken
**sender** *90* Absender
**sensible** *31* vernünftig
**sensibly** *33* vernünftig
**sentence** *8* Satz
**separate** *11* andere/r/s
**serve** *46* servieren, bedienen
**service charge** *46* Bedienungsgeld
**setting** *74* Einstellung
**several** *17p* einige, mehrere
**sheep** *50* Schaf
**shelf** *8t* Regal, Ablage
**shift** *26* Schicht
**shoe polish** *38* Schuhcreme
**shoe shop** *37* Schuhgeschäft
**shop** *6* Laden, Geschäft
**shop assistant** *6* Verkäufer/in
**shop window** *6* Schaufenster
**shoplifter** *35* Ladendieb/in
**shopper** *31* Käufer/in
**shopping bag** *20* Einkaufstasche
**shopping list** *23* Einkaufsliste
**shorten** *76* kürzen
**shortly** *33* kurz
**shoulder** *76* Schulter
**show s.o. round** *6* jdn herumführen
**shrink resistant** *85* nicht einlaufend
**shrink** *85* schrumpfen, eingehen
**side dish** *50* Beilage
**side order** *46* Beilage
**side salad** *46* Salat (als Beilage)
**sign** *58* unterschreiben
**signature (block)** *89* Unterschrift(sabschnitt)
**silk** *67* Seide
**similar** *19* ähnlich
**simple** *35* einfach
**since** *80* seit

**singer** *24* Sänger/in
**sirloin steak** *46* Filetsteak
**sixties** *24* Sechziger
**size** *37t* Größe
**skiing** *24* Skilaufen
**skirt** *77* Rock
**sleeve** *72* Ärmel
**sleeved** *72* ärmelig
**slice** *40* Scheibe
**Slovakia** *63* Slowakei
**smart** *78t* schick
**smoke** *61* rauchen
**sofa** *85* Sofa
**soft drinks** *18* alkoholfreie Getränke
**sole** *80* Sohle
**solution** *87* Lösung
**solve** *80* lösen
**soon** *51* bald
**sound** *40* (sich) anhören, klingen
**souvenir** *57* Andenken
**Spain** *63* Spanien
**Spanish** *13* spanisch
**spare** *24* übrig haben
**special offer** *31* Sonderangebot
**special** *69* besondere(r,s)
**speciality** *46* Spezialität
**specify** *56p* aufführen, spezifizieren
**spell** *52* buchstabieren
**spend** *69* ausgeben
**spices** *18* Gewürze
**spicy** *46* (stark) gewürzt, scharf
**spin dry** *85* trockenschleudern
**spinach** *43* Spinat
**spirits** *18* Spirituosen
**sponge pudding** *44* Biskuitpudding
**spoon** *50* Löffel
**sports shoes** *55* Sportschuhe
**sports shop** *37* Sportgeschäft
**sporty** *78t* sportlich
**sprinkle** *50* streuen
**stairs** *66* Treppe
**stamp** *60* Briefmarke
**standard** *52* Normal
**start out** *69* anfangen
**starter** *46* Vorspeise
**statement** *7* Aussage
**stationery** *65* Briefpapier
**stay** *44* bleiben, übernachten
**steal** *36* stehlen
**stew** *49* Eintopf(gericht); schmoren
**still** *11* (immer) noch
**stock** *8t* auffüllen
**stockings** *77* Strümpfe
**stonewashed** *75* stonewashed
**store** *23* lagern
**store detective** *36t* Hausdetektiv
**straight ahead** *19* geradeaus
**strange** *31* seltsam
**strawberry** *22* Erdbeere
**striped** *72* gestreift
**student** *17* Schüler/in, Student/in
**style** *49* Stil
**stylish** *78t* elegant, modisch
**subject** *89* Thema
**such as** *17* wie zum Beispiel
**suggest** *62* vorschlagen
**suggestion** *87* Vorschlag
**suit** *73* stehen, passen
**suitable** *85* passend
**sunflower seed** *40* Sonnenblumenkerne
**sunglasses** *38* Sonnenbrille
**sunshine** *14* Sonnenschein
**suntan lotion** *67* Bräunungslotion
**supermarket** *6* Supermarkt
**supply** *89* liefern; Lieferung
**sure** *44* sicher
**surfing** *24* Surfing
**surname** *53* Nach-, Familienname
**sweatshirt** *77* Sweatshirt
**Sweden** *63* Schweden
**sweetcorn** *46* Mais
**Switzerland** *63* (die) Schweiz
**synthetic** *72* synthetisch

**T**

**tabby** *24* getigerte Katze
**table** *8* Tabelle
**tablecloth** *65t* Tischdecke
**tablespoon** *50* Esslöffel
**tablet** *37t* Tablette
**tall** *67* groß
**tartan** *73* Schottenkaro
**taste** *37t* kosten, probieren
**tea** *14* Tee
**tea break** *26t* Teepause
**teach** *47* beibringen
**teacup** *14* Teetasse
**teddy bear** *67* Teddybär
**temperature** *72* Temperatur
**tender** *46* zart
**tent** *66* Zelt
**term** *49* Ausdruck
**terribly** *32* furchtbar
**text** *10* Text
**textiles** *65* Textilien
**theatre** *70* Theater
**through** *38* durch ... hindurch, durch
**tie** *67* Krawatte
**tiger prawn** *46* Krabbe
**tight** *75* eng
**tights** *37t* (eine) Strumpfhose
**till, until** *24* bis
**times** *29* mal
**tin** *21* Dose
**tinned** *23t* Dosen-, Büchsen-
**tobacco** *69* Tabak
**together** *24* zusammen
**toilet paper** *22* Toilettenpapier
**too** *31* zu
**toothpaste** *38* Zahnpasta
**top with** *46* belegen mit
**topping** *44* Belag
**tour** *38* Tour
**tourist attraction** *69* Touristenattraktion
**tourist** *71* Tourist/in
**towel** *65t* Handtuch
**tracksuit bottoms** *77* Trainingshose
**trade discount** *89* Händlerrabatt
**traditional** *44* traditionell
**traffic lights** *71* (Verkehrs-)Ampel
**train** *30p* trainieren
**trainee** *6* Auszubildende/r, Praktikant/in
**trainers** *78t* Turnschuhe
**training** *6* Ausbildung, Schulung
**translate** *28* übersetzen
**translation** *28* Übersetzung
**transport** *69* Verkehr(smittel)
**tricky** *47* knifflig, schwierig
**trip** *58* Reise
**trolley** *18* (Einkaufs-)Wagen
**trousers** *39* Hose
**true** *25* richtig
**truly** *90* wahrhaftig
**try on** *67* anprobieren
**try** *30* versuchen
**tub** *38* Becher
**tube** *38* Tube
**tumble-dry** *74* (im Trommeltrockner) trocknen
**tumble-dryer** *74* Trommeltrockner
**Turkey** *63* Türkei
**Turkish** *24* Türkisch
**turn out to be** *82* sich herausstellen
**turn** *19* abbiegen, (sich) umdrehen
**turquoise** *73* türkis
**TV-set** *84* Fernsehgerät
**twice** *24* zweimal
**type** *21* tippen

**U**

**UK, the ~** *63* Vereinigtes Königreich
**under guarantee** *80* mit Garantie
**underground** *27* U-Bahn
**unfortunately** *56p* leider
**university** *9* Universität
**unmarried** *90* unverheiratet
**upstairs** *66* oben
**urgent** *56* dringend
**usual** *56p* gewöhnlich
**usually** *27* normalerweise, gewöhnlich

**V**

**vanilla custard** *40* Vanillesoße
**variety** *40* Vielfalt, Auswahl
**various** *65t* verschiedene(r)
**VAT** *46* MWSt
**veal** *49* Kalbfleisch
**velvet** *54* Samt
**vest** *77* Unterhemd
**vinegar** *40* Essig
**visit** *65t* besuchen
**visitor** *44* Besucher/in, Gast
**vitamin** *37t* Vitamin
**vulnerable** *23* verletzbar

**W**

**waist** *75* Taille
**waiter** *47* Kellner
**waitress** *47* Kellnerin
**walkman** *67* Walkman
**walnut** *40* Walnuss
**washing machine** *65t* Waschmaschine

**washing powder** *18* Waschpulver
**washing-up liquid** *22* Spülmittel
**watch** *33* beobachten; *42* (Armband-)Uhr
**wear** *82* tragen, anhaben
**welcome** *6* herzlich willkommen
**well done** *47* gut durchgebraten
**wheat** *40* Weizen
**whether** *81* ob
**while** *26t* Weile
**wholemeal** *38* Vollkorn-
**wild rice** *46* Wildreis
**willing to** *89* gewillt (sein), bereitwillig
**win** *15t* gewinnen, siegen
**window dresser** *6* Schaufensterdekorateur/in
**within** *52* innerhalb (von), in
**woodwork** *11* Werken (mit Holz)
**wool** *74* Wolle
**work** *35* funktionieren, arbeiten
**worse** *68* schlechter, schlimmer
**worst** *68* am schlechtesten, am schlimmsten
**wrap** *58* (ein)wickeln
**wrist watch** *66* Armbanduhr
**wrong** *20* unrecht haben

## Y

**yet** *82* noch
**yours faithfully** *90* Mit freundlichen Grüßen
**yours sincerely** *89* Mit freundlichen Grüßen

## Z

**ZIP code** *90* Postleitzahl
**zip** *66* Reißverschluss
**zip fly** *75* Hosenschlitz mit Reißverschluss

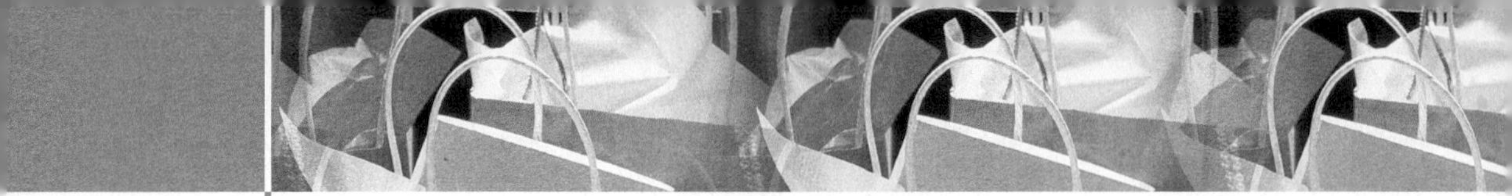

# Basic word list

Diese Liste enthält ca. 400 Grundwörter, die in *Shopping Matters 1* als bekannt vorausgesetzt werden. Nicht aufgeführt, jedoch vorausgesetzt, sind einige elementare Wörter, wie Präpositionen, Pronomen und Zahlen.

**A**

**a lot** viel, sehr
**about** über, ungefähr
**above** über, oben
**address** Adresse
**adult** Erwachsene/r
**after** nach, nachdem
**afternoon** Nachmittag
**again** wieder
**all** alle
**already** schon, bereits
**also** auch, außerdem
**always** immer
**America** Amerika
**animal** Tier
**another** noch eine/r/s, ein/e andere/r/s
**answer** Antwort; beantworten
**any** irgendetwas, irgendwelche(r/s), jede(r,s)
**anybody** jemand, jeder
**anyone** jemand, jede/r
**anywhere** irgendwo, irgendwohin
**apple** Apfel
**around** herum, ungefähr
**arrive** ankommen
**as** wie, als
**ask** fragen, bitten
**aunt** Tante

**B**

**baby** Baby, Säugling
**bad** schlecht, schlimm
**banana** Banane
**bank** Bank, Ufer
**be** sein
**be called** heißen
**beautiful** schön
**because** weil
**become** werden
**beer** Bier
**before** vor, vorher
**beginning** Anfang
**big, bigger, biggest** groß, größer, am größten
**birthday** Geburtstag
**black** schwarz
**blue** blau
**book** Buch, Heft
**boy** Junge
**bread** Brot
**breakfast** Frühstück
**bring** (mit)bringen, holen
**brother** Bruder
**brown** braun
**bus** Bus
**butter** Butter
**buy** kaufen

**C**

**cake** Kuchen
**can** dürfen, können
**car** Auto
**cat** Katze
**cheese** Käse
**child, children** Kind, Kinder
**chocolate** Schokolade, Praline
**cinema** Kino
**city** (Groß-)Stadt
**close** schließen
**club** Klub, Verein
**coffee** Kaffee
**cold** kalt
**colour** Farbe
**come** kommen
**cook** Koch, Köchin, kochen
**could** konnte/n, könnte/n
**country** Land, Staat
**cousin** Cousin/e
**cup** Tasse

**D**

**dark, darker** dunkel, dunkler
**date** Datum
**daughter** Tochter
**day** Tag
**dear** liebe/r
**desk** (Schreib-)Tisch, Schalter
**dialogue** Dialog
**dining room** Esszimmer
**disco** Disko(thek)
**do** tun, machen
**dog** Hund
**door** Tür
**down** (nach) unten, herunter

**E**

**each** jede(r, s)
**early, earlier** früh, früher
**earring** Ohrring
**east** Osten, Ost-
**easy** einfach, leicht
**eat** essen, fressen
**egg** Ei
**e-mail** E-Mail, elektronische Post
**end** Ende
**England** England
**English** Englisch
**Europe** Europa
**European** Europäer/in, europäisch
**evening** Abend
**ever** je(mals), schon (ein)mal
**every** jede/r/s
**everybody** jede/r
**everything** alles
**excuse me** Entschuldigung

**F**

**family** Familie
**fast** schnell
**father** Vater
**fax** faxen, Fax(gerät)
**February** Februar
**feel** (sich) fühlen, der Meinung sein
**female** weiblich
**find** finden, suchen
**finish** (be)enden, aufhören (mit)
**first** erste(r,s), zuerst
**fish** Fisch
**food** Essen, Lebensmittel
**foot** Fuß
**football** Fußball
**forget** vergessen
**free** kostenlos, frei
**Friday** Freitag
**friend** Freund/in
**from** von, aus
**fruit** Obst, Frucht
**fun** Spaß

**G**

**game** Spiel
**German** Deutsch
**Germany** Deutschland
**get** bekommen
**girl** Mädchen
**give** geben
**glass** Glas
**glasses** Brille
**go** gehen, fahren
**go to bed** ins Bett gehen
**gold** Gold
**good** gut
**goodbye** auf Wiedersehen
**gram** Gramm
**grandfather** Großvater
**grandmother** Großmutter
**great** toll, prima
**green** grün
**grey** grau
**group** Gruppe

**H**

**hair** Haar/e
**half** Hälfte, halb
**ham** (gekochter) Schinken
**hamster** Hamster
**hand** Hand
**hard** schwierig, hart
**hat** Hut, Mütze
**have** haben
**help** Hilfe, helfen
**here** hier
**high** hoch
**hobby** Hobby
**holiday** Ferien, Urlaub
**home** Zuhause, Heim
**hope** Hoffnung; hoffen
**hot** heiß, warm
**hour** Stunde
**house** Haus
**how** wie
**how long** wie lange
**hungry** hungrig

**I**

**ice cream** Speiseeis
**idea** Idee
**information** Auskunft, Information(en)
**into** in ... hinein

## J–K

**jeans** Jeans
**job** (Arbeits)stelle, Beruf
**kilo, kilogram** Kilo, Kilogramm
**kilometre** Kilometer
**kitchen** Küche
**know** kennen, wissen

## L

**lady** Dame
**large, larger** groß, größer
**late** spät
**learn** lernen
**leave** abfahren, verlassen
**left** links
**lemon** Zitrone
**lemonade** Limonade
**less** weniger
**let** erlauben, (zu)lassen
**letter** Brief
**like** mögen, gern haben
**line** Linie, Zeile
**list** Liste
**little** klein, wenig
**live** wohnen, leben
**look** schauen, (aus)sehen
**love** lieben, sehr gern mögen

## M

**magazine** Zeitschrift
**make** machen
**male** männlich
**man** Mann
**many** viele
**March** März
**may** dürfen, können
**medium** mittlere(r,s), mittel-
**meet** treffen, kennen lernen
**method** Methode
**milk** Milch
**mineral water** Mineralwasser
**minute** Minute
**modern** modern
**moment** Moment
**Monday** Montag
**money** Geld
**month** Monat
**more** mehr
**morning** Morgen
**most** am meisten
**mother** Mutter
**much** viel
**music** Musik
**must** müssen

## N

**name** Name; nennen
**near, nearest** nahe, nächst
**nearly** fast
**need** brauchen
**never** nie(mals)
**new** neu
**newspaper** Zeitung
**next** nächste/r/s, danach
**nice** schön, nett
**night** Nacht
**normally** normalerweise
**not** nicht
**nothing** nichts
**November** November
**now** nun, jetzt

## O

**o'clock** um ... Uhr
**October** Oktober
**often** oft, häufig
**old, older** alt, älter
**only** nur
**open** öffnen; offen
**orange** Orange; orange
**original** original
**other** andere(r,s)
**over** (vor)über

## P

**paper** Papier, Zeitung
**pardon** Verzeihung
**parents** Eltern
**pay** (be)zahlen
**person, people** Mensch(en)
**phone** Telefon, anrufen
**photo** Foto
**picture** Bild
**pink** rosa
**place** Platz; erteilen
**please** bitte
**pop star** Schlagersänger/in
**post office** Postamt
**potato** Kartoffel
**pound** Pfund, Pfund (Sterling)
**price** (Kauf-)Preis
**problem** Problem
**put** setzen, stellen

## R

**read** lesen
**ready** fertig, bereit
**really** wirklich, eigentlich
**red** rot
**right** rechts, richtig
**road** Straße

## S

**salad** Salat
**salt** Salz
**same** gleiche(r,s), der-, die-, dasselbe
**Saturday** Sonnabend, Samstag
**say** sagen
**school** Schule
**second** zweite(r,s)
**see** sehen
**sell** verkaufen
**September** September
**shall** sollen, werden
**shampoo** Shampoo
**shirt** Hemd
**short, shorter** kurz, kürzer
**shorts** kurze Hose
**should** solle/n, sollte/n
**silver** Silber
**sister** Schwester
**sit** sitzen
**sleep** schlafen
**slow, slowly** langsam
**small, smaller** klein, kleiner
**so** also, damit
**soap** Seife
**sock** Socke
**some** einige, etwas
**somebody** jemand
**someone** jemand
**something** etwas
**sometimes** manchmal
**somewhere** irgendwo, irgendwohin
**son** Sohn
**song** Lied
**sorry** traurig
**soup** Suppe
**south** Süden, Süd-
**speak** sprechen, reden
**sport** Sport
**start** anfangen
**stop** anhalten, aufhören
**story** Geschichte
**street** Straße
**sugar** Zucker
**Sunday** Sonntag
**sweet** Bonbon; süß
**swimming** Schwimmen

## T

**take** nehmen, dauern
**talk** Gespräch; reden
**telephone** Telefon
**tell** sagen, erzählen
**tennis** Tennis
**thank you** danke
**thanks** Dank; danke
**them** ihnen, sie (3. Person Plural)
**then** dann
**there** da, dort, dorthin
**these** diese
**thing** Sache, Ding
**think** denken, meinen, finden
**those** jene
**Thursday** Donnerstag
**ticket** (Fahr-)Karte
**time** Zeit
**toast** Toast
**today** heute
**toilet** Toilette
**tomato** Tomate
**tomorrow** morgen
**tonight** heute Abend/Nacht
**top** oberer Teil, oberste(r,s)
**town** Stadt
**toy** Spielzeug
**travel** reisen
**T-shirt** T-Shirt
**Tuesday** Dienstag

## U–V

**uncle** Onkel
**understand** verstehen
**USA** die Vereinigten Staaten von Amerika
**use** benutzen
**useful** nützlich
**vegetables** Gemüse
**verb** Verb
**very** sehr
**video** Video(film)

## W

**wait** warten
**walk** Spaziergang, (zu Fuß) gehen
**want** wollen
**wash** (sich) waschen
**water** Wasser
**Web site** Webseite
**Wednesday** Mittwoch
**week** Woche
**weekday** Wochentag
**weekend** Wochenende
**well** gut, also
**west** Westen, West-
**what** was, welche(r,s)
**when** wenn, als, wann
**where** wo, wohin
**which** welche(r,s)
**white** weiß
**who** wer, der/die/das
**why** warum
**wife** (Ehe-)Frau
**will** werde(n)
**window** Fenster
**wine** Wein
**winter** Winter
**wish** wünschen
**with** mit, bei
**without** ohne
**woman** Frau
**word** Wort
**work** Arbeit, arbeiten
**world** Welt
**would** würde, würdest, würden
**write** schreiben

## Y

**year** Jahr
**yellow** gelb
**yesterday** gestern
**yoghurt** Joghurt
**young, younger** jung, jünger

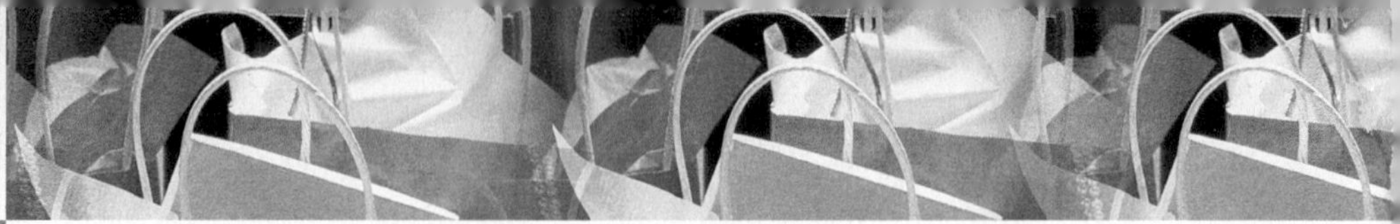

# *Common irregular verbs*

| | | | |
|---|---|---|---|
| **be** | was/were | been | *sein* |
| **become** | became | become | *werden* |
| **begin** | began | begun | *anfangen* |
| **bring** | brought | brought | *bringen* |
| **buy** | bought | bought | *kaufen* |
| **catch** | caught | caught | *fangen* |
| **choose** | chose | chosen | *wählen* |
| **come** | came | come | *kommen* |
| **cost** | cost | cost | *kosten* |
| **do** | did | done | *tun, machen, erledigen* |
| **drink** | drank | drunk | *trinken* |
| **drive** | drove | driven | *fahren* |
| **eat** | ate | eaten | *essen, fressen* |
| **feel** | felt | felt | *(sich) fühlen* |
| **find** | found | found | *finden* |
| **forget** | forgot | forgotten | *vergessen* |
| **go** | went | gone | *gehen* |
| **get** | got | got | *bekommen, erhalten* |
| **give** | gave | given | *geben* |
| **have** | had | had | *haben* |
| **hear** | heard | heard | *hπren* |
| **hold** | held | held | *halten* |
| **keep** | kept | kept | *behalten* |
| **know** | knew | known | *kennen, wissen* |
| **learn** | learnt/learned | learnt/learned | *lernen* |
| **leave** | left | left | *verlassen* |
| **lend** | lent | lent | *verleihen* |
| **let** | let | let | *lassen* |
| **lose** | lost | lost | *verlieren* |
| **make** | made | made | *machen* |
| **mean** | meant | meant | *bedeuten* |
| **meet** | met | met | *sich treffen* |
| **pay** | paid | paid | *(be-)zahlen* |
| **put** | put | put | *setzen, stellen, legen* |
| **read** | read | read | *lesen* |
| **ring** | rang | rung | *klingeln, anrufen* |
| **run** | ran | run | *laufen* |
| **say** | said | said | *sagen* |
| **see** | saw | seen | *sehen* |
| **sell** | sold | sold | *verkaufen* |
| **send** | sent | sent | *senden, schicken* |
| **sit** | sat | sat | *sitzen* |
| **sleep** | slept | slept | *schlafen* |
| **speak** | spoke | spoken | *sprechen* |
| **spend** | spent | spent | *ausgeben, verbringen(Zeit)* |
| **stand** | stood | stood | *stehen* |
| **steal** | stole | stolen | *stehlen* |
| **take** | took | taken | *nehmen* |
| **teach** | taught | taught | *unterrichten, lehren* |
| **tell** | told | told | *erzählen, mitteilen, sagen* |
| **think** | thought | thought | *denken, meinen* |
| **understand** | understood | understood | *verstehen* |
| **wake** | woke | woken | *wecken* |
| **wear** | wore | worn | *tragen* |
| **write** | wrote | written | *schreiben* |